the new tech garden

the new tech garden

PAUL COOPER

MITCHELL BEAZLEY

half title page *detail from a garden at the Festival International des Jardins at Chaumont-sur-Loire, France*
title page *from the Glass Garden designed by Robin Winogrond*
contents page *from the "Voyage of Vitality" garden designed by Bonita Bulaitis*

The New Tech Garden
Paul Cooper

First published in 2001 by Mitchell Beazley, an imprint of Octopus Publishing Group Ltd, 2–4 Heron Quays, London E14 4JP

This paperback edition published by Mitchell Beazley in 2007.

ISBN 978 1 84533 291 4

A CIP catalogue copy of this book is available from the British Library

Executive Editor **Mark Fletcher**
Deputy Art Director **Vivienne Brar**
Project Editor **Michèle Byam**
Design **Amzie Viladot**
Contributing Editor **Richard Dawes**
Production Controller **Jessame Emms**
Picture Researcher **Jo Walton**
Indexer **Laura Hicks**

Set in Grotesque

Printed and bound in China by Toppan Printing Company Limited

CONTENTS

INTRODUCTION: WHY NEW TECH? 6

RADICAL RESPONSES 18

HIGH TECH SOLUTIONS 54

THE KINETIC GARDEN 80

ARCHITECTURAL EXTENSIONS 106

INSTANT GRATIFICATION 138

THE SOFT GARDEN 156

PAUL COOPER GARDEN 184

DIRECTORY OF MATERIALS 189

INDEX 190

ACKNOWLEDGMENTS 192

INTRODUCTION: WHY NEW TECH?

INTRODUCTION: WHY NEW TECH?

A garden is an area of land, usually adjoining a house, and consisting of some or all of the following: a lawn, a mixed border, a shrubbery, a patio, a pool, a path, a pergola, and ornamental features laid out either formally or informally. In addition to the plants, the materials from which it is made are likely to include stone, concrete, and wood. While there are distinct variations, such as gardens found in Asia, notably Japan, this description of a garden is widely accepted in most parts of the world.

But a new generation of garden designers is challenging this traditional concept of the garden and questioning how we make gardens. Working with plastics, metals, glass, and synthetic fabrics, as well as with modern or alternative technologies such as recycling, they are using materials and methods not normally associated with the garden. Many of these gardens are ambitious multi-media and multi-purpose extravaganzas. Some are even instant, others are purely experimental. But what they all share is an exciting, dynamic, and young approach that provides a radical alternative to conventional ideas. Sometimes shocking, always thought-provoking, they are at the forefront of garden design. These are the New Tech gardens.

below A seventeenth-century engraving shows one of the many fountains introduced at Versailles by André Le Nôtre to impress Louis XIV of France. These spectacular water features were made possible by advances in surveying and hydraulic engineering.

"New Tech" is short for "new techniques" and defines a type of garden in which new materials and new working methods, which have contributed to the evolution of a broader concept of the garden, have been adopted. In much the same way the wide availability of iron and glass in the nineteenth century redefined and expanded the possibilities of building styles which had previously been restricted by the limitations of wood and stone.

The use of new or unconventional materials and methods is what marks out the New Tech designers, but theirs is not a singular style of garden design: it embraces a number of new ideas. Many of the gardens reflect the recent diverse developments in contemporary design, and among them are essays in inventive recycling and sophisticated high technology. High Tech, an architectural design style that emerged during the late 1970s, has been particularly influential. The technology-oriented aesthetic of High Tech, with its marked use of industrial materials, has been a source of inspiration for many of the new garden designers.

By contrast, in the late nineteenth century garden makers and designers had adopted the opposite position and totally rejected the rapid industrialization of society. Around the middle of the century architect-engineers such as Sir Joseph Paxton and Maurice Koechlin employed new construction methods and materials to create iron and glass structures such as the Crystal Palace in London and the Eiffel Tower in Paris. It was the era of the great glasshouse, most notably represented by Richard Turner's Palm House at Kew, in London. Advances in heating were allowing the creation of under-cover winter gardens filled with exotic plants, and the conservatory garden was an essential part of the home for prosperous Victorians.

These structures were being erected just as Britain's Arts and Crafts Movement, under its founder William Morris, was about to embark on a creative mission that was to reject mechanization and industrialization in favour of a return to traditional handcrafts. The pioneering English garden designer Gertrude Jekyll, after spending two years at art school, drew upon Arts and Crafts ideas when she began to create gardens in partnership with the architect Sir Edwin Lutyens. By the turn of the century

above *The Palm House at Kew Gardens in London was completed in 1848. Designed by Decimus Burton and Richard Turner, this iron and glass construction pointed to the architecture of the future at a time when garden design in Britain was beginning to look to the past for inspiration.*

she had developed her unique style, with its herbaceous borders and enthusiastic use of wild flowers. Her approach, based on admiration of the "cottage" garden, and combined with Lutyens' taste for vernacular forms and traditional materials and crafts, was essentially old-fashioned and nostalgic. It was to remain popular for decades both in England and abroad.

Perhaps surprisingly, the international Art Nouveau movement, which pervaded most art forms, including architecture, during the final years of the nineteenth century, had little effect on the design of gardens despite the fact that plant forms were its most potent inspiration. Parque Güell in Barcelona, created by the Spanish architect Antonio Gaudí in the first years of the twentieth century, is the exception. In a design that was more low tech than high tech, he used broken, multicoloured pots and tiles to form

abstract mosaic patterns over the surfaces of the garden's organic and curvilinear architecture. The planting is subordinated to the role of a backdrop. Reflecting Gaudí's distinctive style, Parque Güell is unique to the era in which it was created.

It was more than eighty years before another park was designed in a contemporary manner. Conceived by Bernard Tschumi, Parc de la Villette in Paris is based on a simple, hypothetical geometric grid superimposed on the site's irregular shape. Massive, semi-functional, geometric steel structures, all painted bright red but each different, sit at the intersections of the grid lines. An approach to landscape or garden design that is rooted firmly in the present is evident here. The designer may use a modern version of the traditional architectural folly, but little else links the park with the styles of previous periods.

above *One of the four-wheeled tree-transplanting machines that were developed in the Victorian era by the British gardener William Barron. The size of tree that could be moved is impressive even by today's standards. Barron used his innovation to create an almost instant garden on a huge scale for the Earl of Harrington at Elvaston Castle in Derbyshire.*

right *Parque Güell, Barcelona, begun in 1900 by Antonio Gaudí, remains one of the few parks created during the twentieth century to reflect the art and design of its time. The detail shows Gaudí's use of broken, glazed ceramic tiles and pottery to decorate the surfaces of the organic forms of his architecture.*

In the intervening years, the early part of the twentieth century saw garden design generally looking to the past for inspiration. In the USA between the 1880s and the 1920s prosperity and conspicuous consumption led architects to design large country houses with gardens to match, both often in a European period style. In the Netherlands the first two decades of the new century were dominated by the English landscape style and the cottage garden evolved by Lutyens and Jeykll. In Italy, where architects and artists were to play such a leading role in shaping a design language for the twentieth century, garden designers committed themselves to a reworking of the traditional Italian garden.

While garden design in the early twentieth century was to continue to look backwards and become marginalized, a new generation of artists and designers in other disciplines began to look to the future. Inspired by the advances in science and technology, they rejected the past and embraced a redefined art and design that reflected the spirit of the new Machine Age. For some, like the Italian Futurist painters Umberto Boccioni and Giacomo Balla, the motor car was the new icon and speed and dynamism the new subject matter. In Russia another group of artists, led by Naum Gabo and Antoine Pevsner, dispensed with the art of representation altogether in favour of "constructions" in metal, glass, and Plexiglass. By 1919, in Germany, the architect Walter Gropius had rationalized these ideas in an architectural style which was to form the basis of what came to be called "Modernism." Glass, steel, and concrete were the materials of a new aesthetic in which period decoration was replaced by the economic simplicity of modern construction.

By the 1950s, even in traditionally conservative Britain, there was a renewed faith in science and technology. The Festival of

below Thomas Church looked for a new language to solve twentieth-century garden-design problems. This garden, designed for Dewey Donnell at Sonoma, California, illustrates his approach. In most gardens the swimming pool is related neither to the adjacent building nor to the landform. Here, Church has drawn upon the surrounding landscape of winding creeks and salt marshes for inspiration for his fluid-shaped pool.

Les chasubles

left From kinky boots to miniskirts, the 1960s saw a free-spirited and youthful approach to design. The Pop movement embraced fashion, textile, furniture, interior, and graphic design, but despite this popularity there was no sign of the "Swinging Sixties" in the garden.

right This advertisement for Formica from the late 1950s extols the practical and aesthetic advantages of this new laminated-plastic surface covering, which was easy to clean and stain-resistant. Garden design lagged behind other areas of design in that man-made materials were slow to make an appearance.

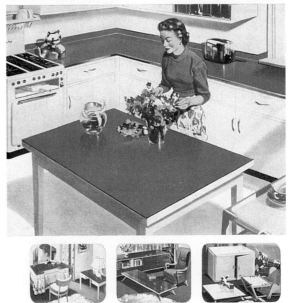

Britain in 1951 celebrated a desire for a style that would reflect the "spirit of the age." In the USA science-inspired decorative motifs were combined with the latest technology. This was the era of Formica, the first fitted kitchens, a number of labour-saving domestic appliances, and the portable radio. Every part of the domestic environment was embellished with contemporary motifs and the latest technology. Everyday objects shaped like molecular models were commonplace. The 1960s and the Pop movement saw a continued faith in technology, but now this was associated with concepts of flexibility and disposability. These radical new ideas, championed by a youth culture with a voice and affluence, challenged the value traditionally placed on longevity. The result was a colourful and vibrant visual style with an emphasis on dynamism and change rather than the status quo. Pop design was popular, fashionable, and affordable and the households of Britain and many other countries were brightened by it. Yet there was no sign of this revolution in the garden. A discrepancy remained between garden style and the rest of the design world.

It has not always been the case that garden design has been out of step with contemporary lifestyle, art, and design. Nor has it always had an aversion to the technology of the day. In Italy during the early seventeenth century the emergence of the Baroque style dictated that the patrons of garden construction, almost entirely ecclesiastics, should be lavish entertainers. At the Villa Aldobrandini in Frascati, near Rome, an extraordinary kinetic illusion was devised: a copper ball was made to appear to dance 1m (3ft) above the pavement – courtesy of a "flow of air" conveyed covertly to a hole beneath.

Towards the end of the seventeenth century advances in science and engineering enabled the French landscape architect André Le Nôtre to fulfil his vision for his patron Louis XIV at the palace of Versailles, south of Paris. The scheme Le Nôtre had in mind required copious amounts of water, a commodity that was in short supply at the chosen location. Thanks to Abbé Picard, an astronomer who had improved surveying instrumentation, it was possible to construct a network of reservoirs. In addition a gigantic pump, which had fourteen enormous wheels that pumped water from the river 162m (530ft) up a hillside to an aqueduct, was built at Bougival on the River Seine. As a result of these endeavours an impressive array of some 1400 fountains was created to entertain the king.

In Britain in the mid-nineteenth century new technology was eagerly adopted to achieve the first "instant" garden. William Barron used new transplanting machines and artificial rocks to create a substantial garden in a comparatively short time at Elvaston Castle in Derbyshire.

From the early years of the twentieth century modern art and architecture responded to the impact of technology on cultural life

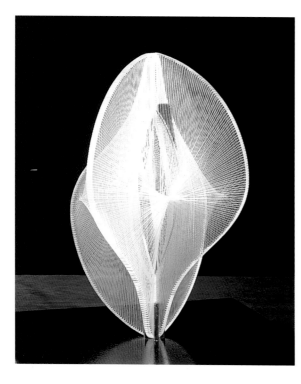

left *One of the "Linear Constructions" made by the Russian-born sculptor Naum Gabo from the 1940s onwards. Gabo used new materials – here Plexiglass and nylon twine – whose visual potential and durability were not exploited by garden designers until decades later.*

below *The Pompidou Centre in Paris, by Piano and Rogers. When the Centre opened in 1977 it heralded the arrival of High Tech design. The use of industrial materials and forms was to influence garden design towards the end of the twentieth century.*

and the environment. Landscape architects and garden designers, however, were slow to react, seeing themselves as closer to nature than to technology. But a response eventually came in the 1930s in the USA, perhaps because there was less of a history of garden design here than there was in Europe. A new approach was first visible in the work of Thomas Church in San Francisco, and then at the Harvard Graduate School of Design, where, in 1938, Walter Gropius became Professor of Architecture. Gropius's Modernist aesthetic of "form for function" and the rational use of modern materials were to influence many of the school's landscape architecture students, among them Garrett Eckbo, Dan Urban Kiley, and James Rose. They looked for new landscape and garden forms to complement the new ideas in architecture and design. What was refreshing was that, instead of applying old styles to new problems, they allowed the problems to generate new forms.

Thomas Church developed his "Californian style" to cope with hillside sites. Wooden decking, bridges, beds, and walls raised for

below *Roberto Burle Marx
trained as a painter in Rio de
Janeiro before turning to
landscape architecture. This
background, together with the
fact that his native Brazil had
no indigenous tradition of
garden design, allowed him to
develop a highly original and
modern style based on the use
of native plants. The complex
sculptural forms of many of
the plants perfectly suited the
demands of the modern
architectural environment.*

sitting emphasized pleasure and low maintenance. It was the
concept of the outdoor living room. Planting was used to
augment living activities – for example, trees for shade and
shrubs for enclosure. Church's rejection of a preconceived
vocabulary of garden forms that were adjusted to suit the
situation, in favour of a modern, problem-solving approach that
takes into account both the site and the client, is central to the
philosophy of today's New Tech garden designers. Dan Urban
Kiley has become one of the USA's leading landscape architects.
Inspired by Le Nôtre's work at Versailles, he reinvented the French
formal style in a manner in keeping with contemporary Modernist
architecture, particularly in his use of water and fountains.

Elsewhere contemporary garden design was in the hands of a
few individuals. In Denmark Carl Sorensen responded to Modernism
by adopting geometric shapes and a restricted planting palette
that excluded flowers. His sunken garden of concentric ovals at
Hellerup, Copenhagen, is a classic example of a modern small
garden. In Britain Christopher Tunnard was almost alone in

interpreting into the landscape the modern architecture of the
1930s. At Halland in Sussex, where he worked with the architect
Serge Chermayeff, he used traditional techniques but in details
and forms that were recognizably modern. More recently,
the garden designer John Brookes, in his work and his book *The
Room Outside* (1969), expounded the idea of the garden as an
outside room. Despite the efforts of such designers, their work
has had limited influence on what is held to constitute a garden.

During recent decades, for most of us the concept of the
domestic garden has changed only in that the garden has become
much smaller. The landscape gardeners of the eighteenth century
worked on a vast scale on private gardens of a size rarely found
now. Today's landscape architects often work on a similar scale
but the clients are mainly public, municipal, or corporate and the
projects are parks, plazas, and motorways. Small private gardens,
for the most part, have been created by their owners in a variety
of borrowed styles, courtesy of popular gardening publications
and of the garden industry of the day.

left *The Viewing Tower, Folly No. P6, one of a series of Neo-Constructivist follies designed by Bernard Tschumi as part of his scheme for the Parc de la Villette in Paris, on which work started in 1982. The park's overall plan, which was based on a superimposed grid, was a radical departure from traditional park layouts.*

In recent years, gardening itself has emerged on both sides of the Atlantic, as a favourite leisure pastime and almost a moral duty. As a result the broader meaning of the garden has been lost to the desire to create colourful mixed borders and explore new horticultural techniques. One factor is the passion for newly discovered, or "invented," plants. This is particularly true in Britain, where a temperate climate allows gardens to be showcases for a wealth of new blooms. Other cultures have very different attitudes to the garden. In China, the home of the world's richest natural flora, plants are appreciated not for their rarity but for their symbolic and literary associations. A Chinese visitor to England in the 1920s even questioned the appeal of the lawn, declaring that it was "Of interest to the cow, but it offers nothing to the intellect of the human being." There have been isolated efforts to promote a modern approach to garden design which is less entrenched in horticulture and in which plants are just one of many materials from which to create a garden, but to date no visible movement has challenged in a concerted way the established view of the garden.

It is not surprising then that the recent change in attitude that has led to the New Tech garden has come about because many of the new generation of garden designers, such as Bonita Bulaitis, have backgrounds in art or design rather than horticulture. In tune with contemporary thought, these garden designers are responding to the pace and challenge of the twenty-first century, bringing confidence in the future and the new rather than retrospection. Their approach does not represent an abandoning of past values such as good plantsmanship; instead it advocates an alternative and more expansive view of the garden that has meaning for the present century and for clients who wish their garden to reflect their modern lifestyle.

The New Tech garden is Modernist in its rejection of tradition and its embrace of innovation. The spirit of Dada and Surrealism is seen in the freedom of its ideas and its more unorthodox expressions. The gardens are individualistic and diverse rather than conforming to one particular style. Designers are showing a willingness to challenge convention and to experiment. The result is gardens that can provide inspiration for us all.

below *Fountain Plaza in Dallas, Texas, designed by the American landscape architect Dan Urban Kiley. The geometry and layout of the scheme are reminiscent of the formal qualities of seventeenth-century French gardens, which Kiley admires. In content, however, the design, with its incorporation of Modernist architectural details, belongs firmly to the twentieth century.*

RADICAL RESPONSES

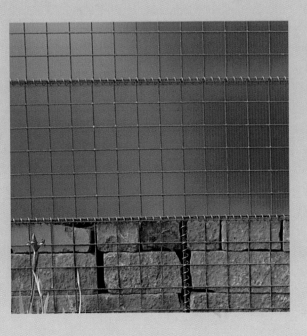

RADICAL RESPONSES

"The shock of the new" was a phrase coined by the Australian art critic Robert Hughes to describe works of art that have challenged our aesthetic values and sensibilities. It might come as a surprise to discover that the paintings of Monet and the Impressionists were regarded with outrage when they were created in the late nineteenth century. One of the first major shocks of the twentieth century was provided by the Dada artist Marcel Duchamp. In 1913 he turned the world of art on its head when he presented an upturned bicycle wheel as a "ready-made" sculpture. His action cleared away in an instant the myths associated with the definition of art and reduced it to simply "an idea." This seemingly negative act was, paradoxically, to provide the opportunity for the more inventive and less inhibited approach to art and design that we enjoy today. For the most part the garden has been exempt from this controversy and unaffected by these liberating ideas. This was because, until recent years, the majority of those who were creating gardens were enthusiastic plant specialists who were either unaware of, or resistant to, radical ideas or design influence.

The latest contributors to garden design have much more varied backgrounds. Some come from other art and design disciplines, while others are from more adventurous schools of landscape architecture – among them Topher Delaney, who trained at the influential Californian School of Garden Design. Others are just mavericks, some of them with no formal training at all. What they have in common is a desire to question all our preconceptions of the garden. They emphasize the art of the garden, or the garden as art, rather than the craft of gardening. They ask: What is a garden? What is it for? How should it be made and what should it be made of? They have even dared to question why a garden should have plants.

In Japan a garden might consist solely of raked gravel and precisely positioned stones, as at Ryoan-ji, north of Kyoto. Here the garden is an arrangement of five carefully placed groups of stones with moss at their bases, in an expanse of raked gravel, a design could be interpreted as islands in a tranquil sea or peaks of consciousness emerging from the unconscious mind.

left Bicycle Wheel, *created by the French-born artist Marcel Duchamp in 1913. This "ready-made" sculpture, consisting solely of two found objects, provoked a more expansionist approach to sculpture, and to art and design in general, that is still in evidence today.*

This garden and similar ones are created for contemplation; as such they are quasi-religious and not intended to be simply decorative. The use of rocks to the exclusion of any substantial planting is not a thing of the past or exclusive to Japan. Very recently, at Revolver Creek in South Africa, in-situ rocks of a different kind were painted with colourful images and patterns to create what its "designer" describes as a "boulder garden." In Europe and the USA a garden which lacked plants would be considered by most people as a contradiction in terms.

below *Andy Goldsworthy has been working closely with the environment for many years. The artist's temporary works using fallen leaves or ice exist only in photographs. This installation, made from stone, is more permanent. It shows that a method of construction usually associated with dry-stone walls can be used to create a sculptural landscape.*

Even more controversial is the fact that some of today's designers are happy to dispense with real plants in favour of artificial ones. Yet this idea is not new either. In the early Islamic gardens of Baghdad there was a fashion for artificial trees. Made of gold and silver, they were often placed in the middle of large pools and had precious stones for fruit. In seventh-century China, in the great park of Emperor Yangdi of the Sui Dynasty, bare trees were decked out with silk flowers in winter. Even in summer real lotus blossom was augmented with fake blooms.

It is easy to dismiss such ideas as frivolous, but when they are considered with an open mind they can encourage us all to be less blinkered in our view of the garden. In particular they can make us more discriminating in the way we use plants. Too often a lack of restraint in the choice of plants, along with a tendency to plant for planting's sake, has produced gardens that are merely

above The wilderness of Revolver Creek, South Africa, was transformed into a colourful landscape by patterns being painted on boulders that were already a part of the terrain. This harsh location has become a garden by the simplest of means – the adoption of natural elements.

a random collection of too many varieties. The result is often confusing and fails to do justice to the plants we admire.

The stimulus for the creation of radically new gardens has come from a redefining of sculpture that has made the medium less object- and gallery-based and more conceptual. During the 1970s many artists chose to leave the confines of the studio to work outdoors. In doing so they entered the traditional domain of the landscape architect, creating works that have been described as land art or environmental art. In 1977, instead of planting trees, Walter de Maria "planted" four hundred 6m (20ft) high steel rods to create his *Lightning Field* in the New Mexico desert. The British artist Andy Goldsworthy has created eloquent temporary works from fallen leaves and turned the craft of dry-stone walling into a way of making sculpture. In 1990 Pierre Vivant trampled the word "past" into a field of poppies and the word "yellow" into a field of oilseed rape.

The lessons of land art and sculptural installations have shaken up the conventional notion of the garden and planting. Jacques Simon's work, for example, includes a floating forest on the River Seine and a European flag "garden" of cornflowers and marigolds. On a lesser scale but more eccentric and owing a debt to the Spanish Surrealist artist Salvador Dali is the *Office Garden*, made by the garden designer Ivan Hicks. The planting is certainly surreal. Instead of growing among rockery stones, sempervivums creep from among the keys of an old typewriter. What is certain about such experiments is that the designers are expanding the definition of the garden. Taken in moderation, their ideas can help us to see the garden in a different light.

Many of the new gardens reflect the influence of Dada and Surrealism, but their anarchy and absurdity are not without historical precedent. Although grander in scale than most modern gardens, the late-sixteenth-century garden at the Villa Orsini in Bomarzo, central Italy, is just as disturbing. Nightmarish sculptured monsters and giants emerge from the undergrowth of a wild and rocky valley left free of any architectural intervention. Interest in this garden was renewed in the twentieth century when Dali was inspired to make a film there. Radicalism in the garden is not new. It has simply been rediscovered.

above This open-mouthed creature is one of the many horrifying sculptures of monsters and giants to be found in the Sacro Bosco, the park to the Villa Orsini, Bomarzo, built between 1552 and 1584 under the direction of Vicino Orsini. The most extreme of Mannerist visions, the garden was very different from any other Italian garden of the period, both in feeling and content, and it still captivates visitors.

right *Ivan Hicks's* Office Garden *owes much to the bizarre juxtapositions of the Dada and Surrealist artists. The structure of the garden is provided by discarded office equipment and other found objects. A typewriter seems about to be digested by a group of houseleeks.*

LIVING SCULPTURE

CHRISTOPHER bRADLEY-hOLE

In this project, created for London's Chelsea Flower Show in 2000, the ground is replaced with water to provide the context for an essay in minimalist design. The garden explores the relationships between old and new as well as between natural, living forms and the inert materials from which the built environment is made.

Christopher Bradley-Hole's inspiration for this garden came partly from his interest in traditional natural materials and a desire to use them in a new way. He was also inspired by nature to make what he calls "an abstract representation of the interrelation of stone, water and plants." The result was a garden in which natural, living plant material and life-sustaining water are combined with inert materials, such as glass and stone, to form what is in effect a three-dimensional walk-through sculpture. This is a minimalist design, a style for which Bradley-Hole has achieved a reputation. He won the award for the Best Garden at the Chelsea Flower Show in 1997 for a similarly reductionist creation. However, it is not this garden's simple abstract plan that makes it so radically different from any that has preceded it at Chelsea. What makes it so eye-catching and thought-provoking is that it seems to have been totally flooded. What remains visible above the water has only been made accessible by the introduction of bridges and decks.

Water occupies the whole rectangular area of the exhibition site, providing a floor for the garden. All the solid elements either emerge from the water or straddle it. Dry-stone walls contain the garden along one long side and one short side. They are not, however, built in the traditional way but formed by four courses of stacked gabions. These are rectangular, galvanized, rust-proof metal cages into which lumps of stone are packed when they are employed in civil engineering in their more conventional role as a land-retaining device. In this garden they have been carefully filled with substantial cuboid blocks of Cotswold stone to provide a modern, minimalist version of the traditional dry-stone wall. Within each cage the stone blocks create an abstract composition

in their own right. Set into the walls at intervals are panels of translucent, acid-etched glass, which let through light and provide visual contrast with the heavy stone of the structures.

The other long side of the garden is open, except for a line of multi-stemmed amelanchiers emerging from small fragments of matching Cotswold stone. The remaining short side is defined by a frame made from large H-section steel beams. These girders are more frequently used out of sight, as the internal structural members of modern high-rise buildings. Here they were chosen because of their plain, functional appearance. Unadorned in any way and free of climbing plants, a 23m (75ft) single beam of the steel structure extends along the full length of the garden to form a central aerial axis.

The design of the garden is symmetrical and this is particularly noticeable in the plan drawing. At each end of the site there is a square wooden deck. One of these is reached by crossing the water on a simple bridge similarly made of wooden planks. The other deck is connected to dry land by a wide path of French white limestone, a feature which adds further textural interest. This stone path cuts into the timber surface and then continues in a large, gentle arc across the expanse of water to link with the wooden deck on the other side. As the path sweeps, in a seemingly weightless manner, along the length of the water, it curves around, and defines the outer edge of, the most substantial area of planting in the garden. The other side of the planted island is a straight edge and lies immediately beneath the steel girder that bisects the garden longitudinally.

Throughout the garden the planting is inspired by natural wetland environments and the island is given over almost

below A semi-opaque glass trough feeds water over a dry-stone wall into a pool within a pool, imparting movement to the garden. In the background a dry-stone wall is given a modern twist. Instead of being stacked in the traditional way, the blocks of stone are carefully arranged in cages made of galvanized steel. Panes of acid-etched glass provide window-like intervals within the wall, their translucence contrasting with the solidity of the stones.

right *In this completely
flooded garden a curving path
of white limestone cuts into
a wooden deck after sweeping
around the back of an island
of wetland grasses. The
uniformity of the island,
the only area of substantial
planting in the garden,
exemplifies the minimalist
philosophy of the designer.*

below *The strap-like leaves
of* Iris kaempferi *in the
submerged wall in the centre
echo the structure of the
multi-stemmed amelanchier
in the front. This planting
scheme is complemented by
an equally considered use of
stone. The small stones in the
foreground give way to walling
stones around the irises and
these in turn become massive
slabs of rock in front of the
island of grasses.*

completely to a mass of moisture-loving grasses. The island looks austere, particularly in its lack of flower and colour. The use of just one type of plant echoes the radical minimalism of the overall design. However, if one looks closely within the mass of grasses it is evident that other plants are present as well. Drawing on his conscientious observation of planting in the wild, Bradley-Hole has perfectly mimicked nature. A walk through a tall grass meadow often reveals more delicate, colourful, and floriferous plants growing in pockets at the base of the grass. In this recreation of a natural wetland the designer has included among the grasses groups of the pink, flowering *Knautia macedonica*.

A further area of planting within the water is more formal and contrived. Planted in an almost totally submerged dry-stone wall that runs parallel to the line of amelanchiers is a row of *Iris kaempferi*. The wall, with its top just visible and in some places disappearing slightly beneath the water, suggests the remains of a landscape that has been recently and deliberately flooded, perhaps to create a reservoir. Near the two wooden decks, and in opposing corners of the garden, two more features inspired by dry-stone walls rise from the water. The stonework of these

sculpture-like forms is more traditional than that of the boundary walls. They are made using the conventional method of dry-stone walling, in which the flat stones decrease in size towards the top. One of the stone "sculptures" is a water feature which is served by a glass trough cantilevered above the walls. Here there is a distinct contrast between old and new. The other dry-stone feature provides symmetry and acts as a simple, informal planter.

One of the most dramatic elements of this garden is the group of massive stones that seem to be sailing in formation across the pool. In plan it can be seen that each stone is cut roughly into the shape of a boat, with bow and stern, and, despite their obvious weight, they add a sense of movement in the calm water. Other movement is provided by natural means as the wind brushes the tall grasses and the iris.

Water played a major part in the design of gardens as long ago as the first millennium BC, when canals criss-crossed the paradise gardens of ancient Persia to create a water feature within a dry landscape. Bradley-Hole's radical twenty-first-century alternative to this long tradition reverses the conventional practice by making the water enclose the land-based elements.

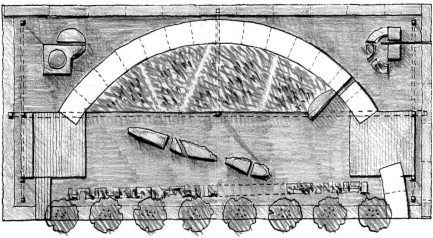

above *The coloured plan reveals a garden that challenges the customary arrangement of water and landscape: the garden is within the water rather than containing it. The drawing also shows the symmetrical arrangement of the garden, in which two identical square areas of wooden decking, one at each end, are linked by a long arc of white limestone blocks. The curving path defines one side of an island of planting, which is truncated on its opposite, straight side by a central axis.*

THE BLUE GARDEN

dAVID sTEVENS

The growth in car ownership and the resultant shortage of on-street parking has caused many front gardens to resemble car parks. David Stevens proves that by a radical rethink the area at the front of a house can accommodate both car and garden. His solution is not for the shy and retiring, however; with its use of bold colours and modern materials, this is a garden for the adventurous and uninhibited.

The front garden has always been a common feature in the countryside, but the urban front garden is mainly a product of the twentieth century. It originated in the "garden cities" of the end of the previous century and within a few decades became an established feature of the fast-spreading suburbs, where affordable semi-detached or detached houses were laid out side by side in avenues, crescents, and culs-de-sac. Consisting of mainly hedges, planting, and lawn, the front garden came to be seen as essential in enlightened social-housing schemes, mainly because it provided separation and privacy from the public highway. Although some keen gardeners used the front garden to show off their horticultural skills, creating impressive floral displays and topiary hedges, most occupants gave it little attention in terms of design. In many housing schemes the layout of the front garden and its planting were determined by the landscape architect responsible for the whole development. In recent years in the UK, mainland Europe, the USA, and elsewhere, however, the role of the front garden as a planted natural barrier between road and house has diminished. With the car now an essential part of modern life, the need for parking space has overridden the need for a garden.

To accommodate one or more cars at home there is often a drive, a garage, and perhaps a parking area as well. In many cases the solution is an area of unrelieved concrete or concrete block paving which makes the garden look like a petrol station forecourt. Much less destructive of the front garden is the solution proposed by David Stevens at London's Hampton Court Flower Show of 1999. His idea welcomes and embraces the car.

The design integrates garden, car, and carport in a manner which is bold yet practical and appropriate. This visually dynamic garden celebrates the car rather than try to camouflage it.

The fluid shapes that dominate the design are inspired by the demands of the car. A brightly coloured and patterned tarmac drive leads the eye towards the house and carport. The roof of the carport doubles as a supporting frame for a cascade of water and planting that projects outwards to a pond to provide a

below *The ground plan reveals a design based on strong curves. These define the drive and are crossed from one direction by a single diagonal line (the screen) and from another direction by a group of diagonal lines (the water cascade and carport). The contrast between the curved and the straight lines gives this bold design its dynamism.*

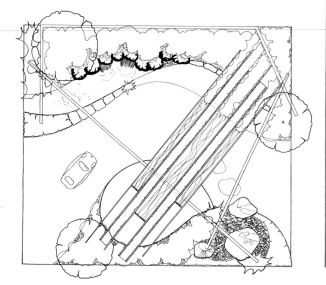

below *A translucent backdrop and strong surrounding colour add a sense of mystery to this curtain of water. Light glimpsed through the darkness invites the viewer to explore what lies beyond. In the foreground the variegated foliage and delicate pink flowers of the hostas are highlighted by the intense blue of the wall.*

spectacular welcome. The cascade cuts through a curvilinear screen that soars diagonally across the garden. Constructed from tubular steel and expanded steel mesh, and reminiscent of the sculpture of the 1960s, the screen aggressively divides the garden in two, separating the private area from the more public, roadside area. The animated water feature that runs along one side of the garden also contributes to this separation in that its sounds help to counteract traffic noise.

The screen is painted bright red and yellow, and primary colours dominate the rest of the garden. There is no place here for pastel tones, even where natural materials are used. The rocks that edge the stream-like water feature are painted a rich blue. (Modern paints make it possible to coat almost anything with durable colours.) The deliberate concealing of the rocks' natural appearance highlights form in preference to texture. It also challenges both the notion of aesthetic taste and the principles of conservation. To some, painting rocks might seem like an act of vandalism; to others it is a refreshing rejection of irrelevant prejudices. But there is no question that this garden makes a

strong case for courageous use of colour. It shows that even the most subtle of natural hues of foliage or flower can be shown to advantage by juxtaposing them with a strong artificial pigment.

The painted rocks also serve to give the garden a sense of make-believe, and it is not hard to imagine the whole scene as a set for a science-fiction movie. A space-age water globe resting on a riverbed of glass marbles does much to create this impression. There is also an element of mystery to the garden. To one side the blue wall is interrupted by a window-shaped opening. A sheet of glass partly obscured by a curtain of water allows a tantalizing hint of what is perhaps another garden beyond this one, just out of reach.

Although the bright colour of the rocks might shock, when it is combined with the equally colourful driveway and overhead structure it creates an environment that counterbalances the car's intrusion. Distinctive architectural plants, such as tree ferns, also provide natural competition, drawing the eye away from the car. This is a garden which in both style and content responds imaginatively to a world where the car is seen as indispensable.

below *Enigmatically, a water globe sits in a river of coloured glass marbles. The dome's reflective surface contrasts with and reflects the textures of the surrounding pine needles and globular beads.*

right *A curving line of rocks painted bright blue leads the eye to a brightly patterned sitting area and, beyond, a drive made of coloured tarmac. The arching fronds of the tree ferns echo the man-made curves of the colourful steel bars overhead, which form a screen that crosses the garden diagonally. The function of the screen is to provide both a real and a psychological barrier between the house and the road.*

ATLANTIS MARIPOSA

hELGA & hANS-JÜRGEN mÜLLER

The desire of art-gallery owners Helga and Hans-Jürgen Müller to create a humanist and ecological paradise inspired them to develop a garden that is a visual feast. Breaking all the rules of conventional garden design, they have produced an idiosyncratic garden full of wonderful ideas, where art and landscape are fused.

In 1984 the Müllers conceived their Atlantis Project. This led to the establishment of a cultural centre that brought together artists, scientists, businessmen, and politicians in an effort to encourage the growth of humanist thinking and ecological awareness. The support of many eminent people, including the Dalai Lama, enabled them to start developing the project at their chosen location at Arona, on the slopes of south-west Tenerife.

Lying off the south-western coast of Morocco, just above the Tropic of Cancer, Tenerife is the largest of the Canary Islands. The climate of the islands is hot and dry, but the surrounding sea has a moderating effect. The peaks of the volcanoes create thermals, upward currents of warm air which cools to form clouds. Rain from these clouds helps to produce a mixed landscape of exotic vegetation among rugged, stony, volcanic slopes. This was the landscape that inspired and influenced the design of the garden

at Arona. The site is in an elevated position on the side of a volcano and offers magnificent views over sea and mountains.

The buildings that constitute the cultural centre are arranged in an irregular manner on different levels along the top of the site close to a road. The land falls away, quite steeply in places, from the buildings. These are quite small and are in the vernacular style, so that they sit unobtrusively amid the natural surroundings. Most of them are made using traditional materials and methods, and among their features are random rubble walls, some rendered and painted in pastel colours, and roofs of thatch or terracotta tiles. But the originality of the place lies not in the individual buildings but in the way they have been arranged to make the most of the topography of the site. Their sensitive positioning provides openings and enclosures that emphasize attractive vistas. They have not been regarded as an isolated entity, an arrogant

right A coloured plan shows the irregular distribution of the centre's buildings along the crest of a sloping site adjacent to a road. Beyond these the garden's informal, curvilinear design unfolds in a series of seemingly random interconnected spaces.

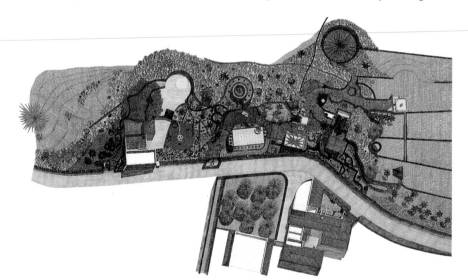

architectural intrusion to which the landscape must conform, but as part of an experiment in landscape design that begins with them, incorporates them, and continues into the stony, sloping garden that lies below.

Indeed one of the major architectural elements is also a landscape feature. It is a series of steps called the Golden Stair which descend from near the Star House and lead down into the garden. Essentially a stony slope, the garden has, in some places, been ordered into formal terraces. Elsewhere it has been treated to give it a more "natural" appearance. Stones and gravels of many sizes and colours are the main ingredients and these are used in a variety of imaginative ways. There are heaps made of fragments of slate, and slopes of scree where stones are carefully deployed according to their colour and size. In some places the gravel makes an informal path, while elsewhere stones and gravel act as a mulch from which the occasional succulent or cactus grows. Larger stones are cemented together to provide more robust walkways, which in some cases are raised. Visiting artists Pompeo Turturiello and Harald Voegele have even arranged stones in sculptural forms.

The garden does not conform to a rigid plan, but instead flows downwards, responding to the contours of the underlying mountainside. Circles and curves dominate the design, which develops into a series of interconnected spaces. For the Müllers it is not, however, the organization of the parts that matters: more important is the content of the individual spaces. The treatment of surfaces and the creation of sculptural and landscape events reveal their preference for detail rather than a concern for the whole. Most modernist mainstream architecture and design follows the opposite principle. But the creators of this landscape are mavericks, rejecting convention in favour of a way of making a garden that has more in common with folk or "outsider" art. It is this vision that makes Atlantis Mariposa so unusual.

The planting is mainly traditional and indigenous and includes pines, palms, aloes, kalanchoes, and cacti. But there are some modern imports, such as eucalyptus. The terraces that flank the Golden Stair are planted with low, carpet-forming ground cover such as prostrate junipers. From among this ground cover there emerges the occasional statuesque cactus. The most effective planting is achieved where the shrubs, succulents, and cacti are positioned in groups or in isolation in a contrasting mulch of coloured stone and gravel. The soft, succulent forms and spiky cacti are set off perfectly by the rough, hard surrounding surface. However, it is the witty, quirky, and imaginative planting of the rotund, yellow, and spiky cacti that best reflects the spirit of the

left One of the many sculptural objects to be found around the buildings and gardens of the centre. This one, by Villaroya and Theisen, is made of thatch and adds further textural interest to an environment of rendered walls and large cobblestones. To the right a door surround made of stones frames a view of the landscape beyond.

right A group of yellow cacti form an orderly line on a bed of red stones. Above, on a raised terrace, a tree-like succulent stands in isolation, its shape highlighted by both the dark background and the coarse white gravel at its base.

place. The way in which these have been planted seems to have animated them. Looking like little porcupines, they appear to be scurrying freely up and down the slopes. In another place they form an orderly line. This eccentric approach to planting is just one of the many unexpected landscape features that give this garden its unique character.

Spaces throughout the site are enlivened by artworks and unorthodox landscape garden elements. Among these are coloured glass marbles set into the floor of a small courtyard, and a puzzling large, semi-conical, thatched object that rests against a rendered wall. Then there is Red Square, which is actually oval and is "paved" with rough red stones. In the middle is a white pebbled pool fed by a small artificial spring. On one of the flatter areas in the garden stones of different colours are cemented together to form a hard floor decorated with a simple flower-motif mosaic. This design is a tribute to the traditional flower paving practised by the peoples of the Iberian peninsula. All around there are visual events, many involving interaction between art and nature. A fig tree has its trunk and branches painted bright blue. An angular, almost prickly sculpture by Hans-Jürgen Müller stands next to a real cactus. Elsewhere a cactus has been grown and manipulated into human shape. The landscape of Atlantis Mariposa is full of such surprises.

THE KUHLING GARDEN

tOPHER dELANEY

This garden design for a house in a suburban street in Palo Alto, California, provided an alternative, contemporary, and customized solution for a client who wished his garden to be a tranquil place conducive to contemplation.

A wide path of polished black granite leads to the main entrance of the house, passing through two borders planted exclusively with Irish moss, *Helxine soleirolii*. Nestling in these low beds are glass "rocks" which glow at night, thanks to concealed fibre-optic lighting. As well as adding atmosphere, they help to light the path to the front door. Another path, narrower and of black concrete, weaves its way through the planting to the side of the house.

The design is a radical alternative to the conventional front garden and is at the same time very simple. Its arresting look was achieved through the interplay of three textures: a hard, smooth walkway, soft, delicate planting, and the shiny angularity of glass. This front garden offers a thought-provoking welcome. In most similar sitations, however, little is done to engage the visitor. Usually given over to lawn, driveway, and the occasional hedge and planted area, they have little meaning for owner or visitor. In the great gardens of the eighteenth and nineteenth centuries the long driveway from the main gate often took a circuitous route

to both give a sense of scale and to present the house, when eventually seen, in the best context. A large terrace in front of the house provided a place where guests could be received and from which they could admire the impressive views. As private houses became smaller and more numerous, and land more precious, the importance of the front garden was lost. The role of this small front garden, tucked behind a camellia hedge and therefore invisible from the busy road, is altogether different. It is intended to act as a buffer zone between the client's working life in the city and his home. The combination of glass "rocks" and moss is a soothing antidote to his high-pressure work. Topher Delaney specializes in gardens that are custom-built to suit the personality of each of her clients, and this is what she has achieved here.

The front garden is connected to the rear garden by the continuation, through the house, of the black-granite paving used for the path at the front. The dominant colours in the front garden are the black of the path and the dark green of the moss. In the rear garden blue and gold predominate. The first comes in the form of a long, low wall that defines the patio at the rear of the house and is painted in shades of lavender blue. This colouring is echoed by two parallel blocks of lavender hedges that run alongside the wall. The wall and hedges form one side of the courtyard that has been created in the small – about 12m x 20m (40ft x 60ft) – back garden. There is also an area of lavender and gravel at the far end of the garden, cut off from the main courtyard by a high screen. This tapering triangle of land is

left *In the front garden translucent "rocks" of blue glass with intriguing shapes sit on a lush, green bed of Irish moss. Lit internally, they emit a cool, slightly mysterious glow which, at night, illuminates the path leading to the front door.*

below *The front entrance to the house is recessed and is reached by a path of black granite wide enough to form a courtyard-like area. Continuing in the same material, the path passes through the house and re-emerges at the rear, where it opens out into a seating area. Flanking the path at the front are two planting borders entirely given over to Irish moss. On this sit pieces of blue glass which give out a gentle glow, courtesy of fibre-optic lighting. A narrow, serpentine path of black concrete, "The Scholar's Walk," runs through the planted area.*

right *This water feature graces the rear garden. On an obelisk of natural rock sits a delicate elliptical glass saucer filled with bubbling water. The pale blue of the glass is mirrored in the nearby mass planting of lavender and the blue wall that defines the patio.*

below The ground plan shows the front and back gardens, to right and left respectively, and their relationship to the house. The single colour and texture of Irish moss dominate the front garden, while in the back garden the colour scheme is lavender blue and gold.

described by the designer as a "cloister," and its high screen on one side and a sentinel-like row of cypress trees on the other do give it an almost architectural presence.

The gold colouring in the courtyard comes from a combination of golden gravel, soft, pinkish-gold stone paving, and, most notably, two large, free-standing stucco walls painted a rich dark gold. Their impact is heightened by the positioning of a plain stone bench and a single natural stone nearby, together with simple terracotta pots containing evergreen citrus and guava plants. The walls sit to one side of the courtyard garden and provide a dramatic focal point. One wall could also have a functional role: it is L-shaped and might be used to screen off any of the more mundane features that are necessary in a practical garden. Behind the other wall an open area contains more terracotta pots of citrus and a simple water feature, blue like the nearby lavender. This consists of a natural-stone obelisk that supports a shallow, blue-glass saucer of bubbling water. One wall is square, while the other is rectangular, but in their colour and geometry they are both intended to pay homage to the famous Mexican landscape architect Luis Barragán. As well as evoking the vibrant colours of his native city of Guadalajara, Barragán's work contains strong references to the indigenous buildings of the Mediterranean and displays Muslim influences.

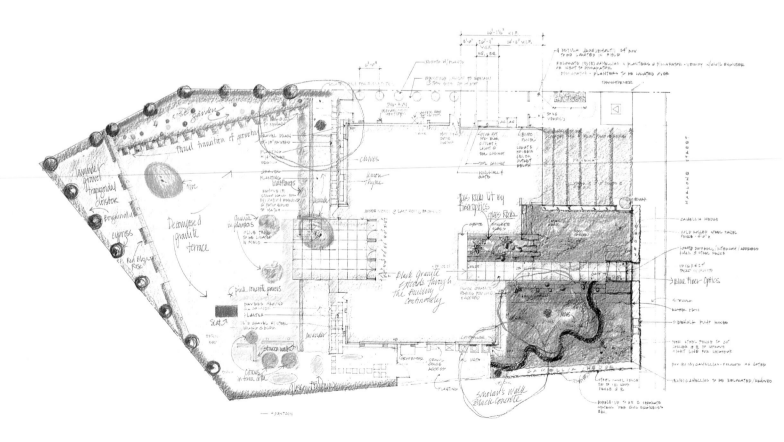

The remaining two sides of the courtyard are defined by tall metal screens, which have both an aesthetic role and a practical one in giving privacy. The principal screen runs the full length of the long side of the courtyard, and has at its base a low, stucco wall painted in the same lavender blue as the wall that surrounds the patio. Along the length of the screen is a series of five equally spaced and precisely made openings, each differing in width from the adjacent one by 30cm (1ft). As the size of the openings decreases, the height of the screen increases, from 2.5m (8ft) at the low end to 4.5m (15ft) at the high end. This complex geometry creates a series of unequal apertures through which the sun casts ever-changing shadows. The serene progress of these

darker bars across the golden horizontal plane of the courtyard provides a calm environment in which to sit. The screen itself is not left bare, however. Its straight lines are softened by masses of brightly coloured flowering climbers, including red roses and trumpet vine. The screen beyond the "cloister" is planted with bougainvillaea, and all these flowering plants add yet another wash of colour that recalls the vivid palette of Barragán.

At night the garden is given another dimension. Just as the illumination of the glass rocks adds a touch of theatre to the front garden, so lighting dramatically enhances the deep-gold walls of the back garden. They glow in the dark, and as the surrounding trees are silhouetted, the scene is one that invites quiet reflection.

above At dusk, uplighting heightens the rich gold colour of the large, asymmetrical walls. Pinkish-gold concrete slabs and golden gravel add to this effect, which causes the bed of lavender and the blue wall on the left to fade from view. Evergreen citrus and guava plants in square, terracotta pots echo in miniature the trees to the rear.

ODENWALD GARDEN

SIEGFRIED & ri SPECKHARDT

A husband-and-wife team of an artist and a plantswoman have together designed a sculpture garden with a difference. Here the sculpture is not a collection of isolated pieces set against a backdrop of planting. In this unusual collaborative garden sculpture and nature go hand in hand.

The garden belongs to its creators, Siegfried and Ri Speckhardt, and is situated in Odenwald, near Heidelberg, in the Rhine Valley. Ri Speckhardt is a true plantswoman and is sensitive to the garden's location in a spectacular part of Germany dominated by river valleys and forests. She has used ferns and shade-tolerant plants to make it feel akin to the dense woodland that surrounds it. However, this is not a garden just for plant lovers. It is also a sculptor's garden. Siegfried Speckhardt is an artist who makes sculpture and artefacts out of reclaimed and found objects, many of which occupy the garden. His sculptures and constructions are an integral part of the garden, sharing space with the planting designed by his wife.

The main gates to the house and garden give the visitor an inkling of what to expect beyond. Although made of iron, they bear no resemblance to the decorative garden gates traditionally made by blacksmiths. These are usually of forged metal shaped into organic, heraldic, plant-based, or, more recently, abstract patterns, but here the gates are fabricated from a variety of metal parts. Their construction includes a pair of small, cast-iron wheels at the centre to support their weight and to help them open and close freely. Attached to the frame, made of angle iron and welded steel mesh, are various found objects, including a large blade from a wood-cutting circular saw, perhaps a reference to forestry. With a touch of wit, a spanner forms the latch and the gates are topped by a bicycle wheel which seems to serve no function.

Unwanted household objects, along with items from local demolition sites and scrapyards, provide Siegfried with the raw materials for his work. Metal, stone, and wood are frequently combined in multi-media constructions. Like the gates, a number

below *A blue-painted, temple-like construction is the centrepiece of this garden surrounded by woodland. Made from scrap metal, including sheets of steel mesh and found objects, the work is gradually being colonized by the encroaching vegetation. To the left a vibrantly coloured sculpture stands out against the cool green planting.*

of the constructions are not free-standing sculptures. Often their role is to provide architectural interest in the garden.

Colour is an important element in many of the sculptures and constructions. In some cases it unifies different materials and forms, while elsewhere it identifies and highlights shape. Blue is one of Siegfried's favourite colours, the "colour of the sky and fantasy." A dark-blue temple is the garden's focal point, and the garden furniture is painted in the same shade. Red, says the artist, represents "fire and life," and this is the colour of the spheres that adorn the "chandelier" hanging from the top of the temple's simple cupola. An open structure, often used for temporary exhibitions, the temple at one time housed the remains of a theatre set designed by Siegfried.

The temple is made of reclaimed pipes and tubular steel and has screen-like walls of welded steel mesh, which is normally used to reinforce concrete slabs and roads. There is also Siegfried's trademark bicycle wheel, which can spin on one of the projecting tubes, possibly a homage to the French Dadaist Marcel Duchamp. The temple sits within a random stone wall. Ivy is allowed to attach itself to the blue frame and inevitably the structure will eventually be clothed in planting. This does not seem to concern its creator. In fact many of the artworks in the garden interrelate with the natural environment or even merge into it. Some

sculptural pieces are attached to the plants. For example, colourful metal ribbons hang from ferns, providing them with artificial flowers and decorating them just as one might a Christmas tree. In effect they are jewellery for plants.

Much of the humour of the pieces stems from a play on the relationship between plants and sculpture. A stone head of a lioness on top of a pillar in the courtyard near the house is accompanied closely by her mate, also in stone but with a mane made of a growing ivy. The ivy offers a further surprise: strange little faces peer out of it. In another work expanded-metal mesh is fashioned into multicoloured, palm-like leaves. These, combined with a central trunk and a mass of twisted wood and red, berry-like spheres, make a deliberately poor imitation of a plant. Nearby a tin can and a chunk of roughly carved wood have been brought together to create a more easily recognizable bird.

A pond is surrounded by moisture-loving plants, across which there is a ramshackle deck made from rough-cut tree trunks and branches. Fixed to an equally rustic and insecure-looking handrail are all manner of found objects, including a large spring, chains, and a handle-less spade. A sculptures made from two bicycle wheels provides an unorthodox support for plants, its radiating spokes perfect for twining shoots. Some of the sculptures are made of weathered wood or stone and a few of the metal

below *Making use of discarded bicycle wheels, Siegfried Speckhardt has created an amusing sculpture which is about to become a support for nearby climbing plants. The rusting metal construction also elegantly frames a group of foxgloves.*

left *Expanded-metal mesh, brightly coloured in green and yellow, has been cut and shaped to form the leaves of what appears to be a metal palm tree. The sculpture sits in a planted landscape of ferns and elder bushes that form the woodland edge of the garden.*

sculptures have been allowed to rust. The natural colour of these works makes them almost invisible in the planting. Many will almost certainly deteriorate and decay as part of an intentional recycling process by which they will return to nature.

The garden is filled with perennials and ferns, the latter providing an excellent foil for many of the sculptures. The rich, green foliage contrasts well with the colours that Siegfried uses in his work. A large area of the garden is shaded for most of the day, and this orientation, together with the moisture provided by the nearby stream, makes it ideal for moisture-loving plants such as ferns. *Matteuccia struthiopteris*, the shuttlecock fern, and *Osmunda regalis*, the royal fern, thrive alongside flowering moisture-lovers such as rodgersia, astilbe, ligularia, and aruncus.

These conditions also favour hydrangeas, which thrive here, producing huge leaves. Where the sun does touch the garden, Ri has planted herbs, including many lesser-known species, such as Japanese basil and Vietnamese coriander.

Siegfried's sculptures belong more to folk art than the world of modern sculpture, even though their form and structure owe a debt to the work of the French-born artist Marcel Duchamp, the Constructivists, and the kinetic creations of the Swiss sculptor Jean Tinguely. They are neither more nor less important than the planting created by Ri. It is the intimate relationships between plantswoman and sculptor, and between art and nature, along with a great sense of fun, that make this garden fascinating for the visitor and invest it with meaning for its creators.

above Close to the stream and pond, Siegfried has combined tin cans, carved wood, and stone to create fantastic creatures that seem to have just emerged from the luxuriant planting of ferns and other moisture-loving plants.

THE TOUCHY-FEELY GARDEN

eMILY aULT

Making a garden for an autistic child calls for a radical rethink of both the function and content of a garden. Emily Ault had no professional experience in designing gardens but this did not prevent her from creating a magical environment that is safe and stimulating for her son George and is enjoyed by all of her three children.

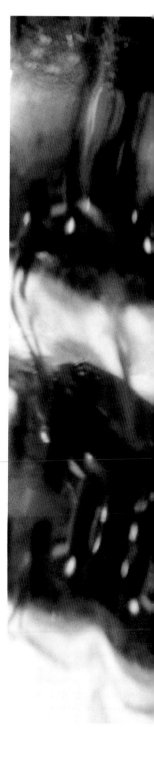

Seven-year-old George's severe learning difficulties meant that an ordinary garden would be of little benefit to him and could be full of dangers. Advised that he needed as much stimulation as possible if he was to develop, his mother set out to build an imaginative garden that would both stimulate him and be a safe environment in which to play. It would also have to satisfy her other children, a son aged ten and a daughter aged three.

Emily noticed that George was fascinated by the patterns he noticed on the ground in the pavement, the road, or the park, and she remembered this when it came to choosing hard landscaping surfaces. She could have used the colourful rubber safety flooring designed for playgrounds, but felt that its uniform texture was uninteresting. Instead she used terracotta bricks to define paths that weave their way through the garden. These are set within a random arrangement of various-sized slabs of York-type stone which display plenty of variation in colour and texture. Elsewhere surface interest is created with black engineering bricks laid in a basket-weave pattern.

A brick path goes under an iron archway and passes a water feature. A favourite of George's, this was designed and made by Fish Bros, a London-based collective of sculptors. Shaped like a tall mushroom, it stands 1.5m (5ft) tall. Six steel legs support a sort of conical hat made from beaten copper. Water is pumped up a central pipe and cascades down the hat. From here it runs on to chains, chimes, and horseshoes, creating wonderful sounds. Finally

left *Sunlight shining through coloured plastic insets in a trellis screen makes patterns on the stone paving, providing stimulation for George, the autistic child for whom this garden was created.*

This fascinating image of the garden is created using a readily available version of the distorting mirrors used in funfairs. Several of them are fixed to the garden fence. George loves looking into them and is excited by the patterns the reflected light makes on the surrounding walls and paving.

it drops into a reservoir filled with pebbles and green and blue spheres which is attractively illuminated at night.

Because George is interested in anything that opens and shuts, Emily built him a gazebo in purple trellis. In the wall is a window with a bead curtain and from a doorway hangs a silver-flecked plastic shower curtain that George can push himself through. The gazebo is topped by a "cupola" of chicken wire, through which are threaded crystal beads that resemble raindrops.

George also likes to see light patterns on floors and walls. Set into gaps in the trellis panels are squares of transparent coloured plastic, and when the sun shines through the trellis, coloured shapes are projected onto the ground. Emily has hung unwanted compact discs from an apple tree, where they sway in the breeze, providing a dazzling play of reflected light. To fences or pieces of trellis she has attached distorting mirrors made from plastic, which add to the garden's daytime light show.

George tends to try to eat anything he comes in contact with, so the Royal Horticultural Society helped Emily to formulate a list of safe plants. Growing in gaps or pots are fragrant herbs such as rosemary, sage, bergamot, santolina, camomile, lavender, and thyme. Other plants with colourful, fragrant, or unusual flowers were introduced, including *Eryngium gigantium* (giant sea holly), passion flower, jasmine, and violas. The grass *Molina caerula* and an agave were chosen for their interesting texture or shape. George has nicknamed the agave "the prickle plant."

The Touchy-Feely Garden, as it is fondly known, has made George more independent and he can now play safely without his mother's constant attention. His brother and sister love it too.

left *A gazebo-like room made from trellis, and complete with a bead-curtained window and a door made from a shower curtain, was designed in response to George's love of windows and doors. The materials used here and throughout the garden were chosen to provide a safe and stimulating environment for him to play in.*

right *Aware of George's interest in surface patterns, his mother had terracotta bricks laid end to end to form paths that wind their way through an area paved with York stone-type slabs. The paths look inviting and have proved popular with all three children, who enjoy using them as cycle tracks.*

THE SPLICE GARDEN

mARTHA sCHWARTZ

An inhospitable roof terrace in Cambridge, Massachusetts, provided a challenge for the American landscape architect and artist Martha Schwartz. Her imaginative solution subverts our usual notion of a garden as a place for growing plants. What appears to be a garden of topiary and clipped hedges is not all that it seems.

The 8m x 10m (24ft x 30ft) rooftop space belongs to a nine-storey office building that houses the Whitehead Institute for Biomedical Research, a microbiology centre. *The Splice Garden* was commissioned as part of an art collection put together by the centre's director, David Baltimore.

The high walls that enclose the courtyard-like terrace made it dark and uninviting. A further problem was that the floor was not strong enough to hold much additional weight. Containers with a sufficient depth of soil to grow plants would be too heavy, and in any case there was no water supply to the rooftop and little money in the budget for maintenance of a garden. For these reasons it was out of the question to use living plants. Even so, it was clear that this space, overlooked by a classroom and faculty lounge, could be made into a pleasant area where the centre's staff could sit and eat in the open air.

The easiest way to have made the space both more attractive and more usable would have been to introduce hard-landscape features that would simply improve upon what was already there. These might have included wall decoration, a decked floor, and comfortable seating. But, because the site made it impossible to create a real, planted garden, Schwartz decided instead to construct an imaginary one by providing signs or signals to suggest a garden. For her "the strategy at Whitehead [was] to create a garden through abstraction, symbolism and reference."

left A view of the "splice," the line along which two gardens appear to have been cut and then joined. On the left side of the splice is a garden in the formal French Renaissance style; on the right is a surreal Japanese Zen garden. The truncated circular "box hedge" is the principal device in this illusion.

In this disturbing transformation of a traditional Japanese Zen garden a clipped topiary "pompom" replaces the customary standing rock and the usual raked gravel has become bright green.

All the "plants" in this garden are fake. The clipped box hedges, which double as seats, are made of rolled steel covered in Astroturf. Green gravel and green paint help to reinforce the illusion that this is a planted garden.

Schwartz also made the garden convey a theme relating to the work of the Whitehead Institute: genetic engineering. She gave it a name inspired by the process known as gene splicing, by which DNA fragments with the required activity are isolated and spliced into DNA from a host organism. In simple terms, two different entities are cut and joined together permanently. The garden plays with the idea that there are risks in this research, notably the possibility of creating monsters. For this garden is a sort of monster, like a creature that one might find in the house of horrors at a funfair. It consists of not one but two gardens, joined together like Siamese twins. But in this instance the twins are far from identical. They are from very different cultures, and in addition variations have occurred that suggest some experiment in cross-fertilization that went wrong.

One side is based on a formal French Renaissance garden, the other on a Japanese Zen garden. But the elements that compose these two garden styles and are traditionally identified with them have been mixed to surreal effect. The rocks usually found in a Zen garden have become topiary pompoms from the French garden: some of this "fake" topiary is suspended and projects horizontally from the green wall. In the French garden the artificial clipped box hedges have palms and conifers unexpectedly "growing" in them.

A circular box "hedge" is truncated sharply and slightly off centre, to create the illusion of an imaginary pane of glass that seems to divide and yet join the two gardens. The box hedges that butt up to this divide reinforce the trompe l'oeil. In effect this dividing line is the "splice" where the two gardens are joined.

Schwartz's adventurous use of artificial plants rather than real ones questions the idea of a garden as a space that contains living plants. Yet it is her use of plastic plants rather than her omission of real ones that most challenges our perceptions, for, although it is illusory and even surreal, the site still looks like a garden. In developing this deception she has created both a highly unconventional garden and a work of art.

right *References to box hedges, clipped topiary, and raked gravel, along with the predominance of the colour green, work together in this composite garden to suggest a real garden. In fact all the "plants" are fake. The clipped box hedges are made of rolled steel covered in Astroturf and serve as both visual elements and seats.*

HIGH TECH SOLUTIONS

HIGH TECH SOLUTIONS

For most of the twentieth century garden designers displayed an aversion to the increasing dependence on technology, even though modern science had been instrumental in the creation of new plants and helpful in their subsequent maintenance. For this reason it is surprising that when garden design did embrace the aesthetics of the industrial world it was to be inspired by the most futuristic of contemporary design languages: High Tech. A fusion of high style and modern technology, this radical approach to design was characterized in architecture by the use and display of high-precision engineering. The services of buildings were exposed for all to see. Air ducts and piping, for example, were highlighted (often with bright paint), not concealed as formerly. In interior and domestic design the fun of High Tech lay in finding everyday uses for specialized industrial products. Dimpled rubber safety flooring was used as wall covering. Aluminium floor plates were applied to all manner of surfaces, horizontal and vertical.

This appropriation of ready-made industrial components and materials in order to create a new technological aesthetic was characterized in popular culture by perforated steel-sheet furniture, graph-based wallpapers and fabrics, and bulkhead-type lighting. In the more exclusive and design-conscious retail outlets High-Tech style was less restrained. Even armchairs, usually associated with soft, padded fabric or leather, could be found that were constructed of moulded plastic, glass, or even metal mesh.

In architecture High Tech is exemplified by the work of the Richard Rogers Partnership, which designed the Lloyd's Building in London and the Pompidou Centre in Paris. Both buildings are identifiable as high tech by their machine-like, industrial appearance. Their services are left undisguised on the external elevations and the Lloyd's Building even has permanently installed cranes to maintain and service its complex vertical structures.

One of Rogers's partners, John Young, applied this style to the design of his own penthouse apartment beside the River Thames in Hammersmith, London. This celebration of Le Corbusier's idea of the house as a "machine for living" encapsulates High Tech. Many of its details are taken from the aeronautical and marine industries, and include aircraft landing lights and gleaming ships'

above *Shiro Kuramata's 1986 armchair rejects padded upholstery for a springy, nickel-plated, expanded metal. While the transparent, lightweight look is a long way from the archetypal bulky easy chair, the design illustrates the potential of employing industrial materials.*

wheels from ocean-going yachts. If there is an overriding theme it is one inspired by ships and lighthouses. This is most in evidence on the exterior platforms. Free of any temptation to introduce plants – hardly appropriate in any case to a nautical environment – Young incorporated on the upper "deck" a glazed observation room. On a lower terrace a circular wall of glass bricks houses the master bathroom. When this room is lit at night the cylindrical structure glows like the lantern of a lighthouse. Elsewhere on the terraces, white railings and air-vents suggest a ship's deck.

More than twenty years since the Pompidou Centre appeared like a spaceship from another world among the eighteenth-century buildings of Paris, the High Tech movement is still going strong, particularly in Britain. Much of the enthusiasm for the style is due to the fact that it brought to modern design a sense of dynamism and a new decorative vocabulary that was unrestrained and full of visual metaphors.

But, despite its popularity, High Tech has only recently found its way into the garden. The style's hard-edged and often highly

above This pyramidal sculpture, designed by the garden designer David Stevens, combines stainless steel, water, and tulips. The steel's hard edge and highly reflective surface are animated by the thin film of water that passes over the pyramid and contrast well with the delicate flowers.

left *Hemispherical roof lights are allowed to mix with the planting in this roof garden designed by Dan Pearson. Nestling among grasses, ferns, and thrift, these clear-plastic domes, with their science-fiction appearance, give the garden an unorthodox sculptural interest. The idea of contrasting high tech with natural elements is simple but the effect is stunning.*

right *John Young's design for his own penthouse apartment is an essay in High Tech. Drawing on nautical imagery, the upper "deck" has its own glass-and-steel lookout post. After helping to revitalize architecture in the late 1970s, High Tech is now influencing garden design.*

reflective materials might seem alien in a planted environment. But it is this striking juxtaposition that garden designers are finding interesting. Far from corrupting the garden, these new materials are seen as complementing plants' softer, organic textures and forms. The use of High Tech materials instead of brick, stone, and wood brings a visual dynamism to the garden. Mirror-like surfaces, for example, add an extra dimension to colour and pattern. In a roof garden he created for the 1996 Chelsea Flower Show Dan Pearson introduced cylindrical, stainless-steel containers planted with a contrasting natural and informal grouping of birches and grasses. On the roof garden's "floor" he allowed the bubble-like roof lights to be part of the planted border.

It is not just a new aesthetic that High Tech has brought to the garden; there are also practical benefits. Multicoloured rubber flooring can be used instead of grass to provide an all-weather, all-year recreation area. It does not need cutting – just vacuum-cleaning. Easily maintained surfaces and computer-controlled watering systems can provide the less enthusiastic gardener with an almost labour-free garden. High Tech materials and products are often lightweight, easy to handle, and clean compared with bricks and mortar. Therefore they can easily be carried through the house, if necessary, and are particularly suitable where access is difficult. High Tech's many aesthetic and practical advantages make it easy to see why it is helping to shape the modern garden.

SHOWA MEMORIAL PARK

fUMIAKI tAKANO

Tokyo's Showa Memorial Park is one of the few public parks to have been created in the twentieth century. What is also significant about this space, the largest urban park in Japan, is that much of it is dedicated to children and play.

It is only recently in the history of the public park that areas have been designated for play and recreation, in order to meet the needs of children living in urban environments. In most cases areas within landscaped and picturesque parks were simply set aside for sports activities or converted into play areas equipped with facilities such as swings and slides. The inclusion of these play elements was driven by a change in the social climate in the middle of the twentieth century, when it was no longer seen as acceptable for children to play in the streets near their homes. At that time many houses had no private garden, and when high-rise accommodation became widespread the need for designated play areas grew even more pressing. The growth of road traffic also made it desirable to provide safe play areas.

Many such areas were created on reclaimed plots of land as a part of urban redevelopment, since by the twentieth century large public parks were generally in decline, having been either neglected or upgraded to include more decorative civic floral displays. In Britain this latter usage was largely inspired by the Britain in Bloom competitions, which encouraged local authorities to create spectacular but temporary displays at the expense of providing more worthwhile facilities.

The history of the public park in Britain and Europe began when open spaces were made accessible to the public, usually by royal or aristocratic largesse, as public promenades. In London, for example, royal parks such as Hyde Park and Richmond Park were opened to the public, although in the case of Regent's Park neither seats nor shelters were provided for pedestrians, perhaps to discourage those without carriages. It was J. C. Loudon who, in the nineteenth century, first advocated the idea of the public park, which he thought could "raise the intellectual character of the lowest classes of society." The public park as an aspect of social

below A screen of shrubs and trees defines the boundaries of this play area, designed by the Takano Landscape Planning Co. Ltd, in Showa Memorial Park. A complicated labyrinth is delineated on the ground but the lines do not suggest any particular direction that children's games should take; the choice is left to them. Various artefacts, including a low, pyramid-like structure, are distributed about the play area, and again children are free to use these in their play as their imagination guides them.

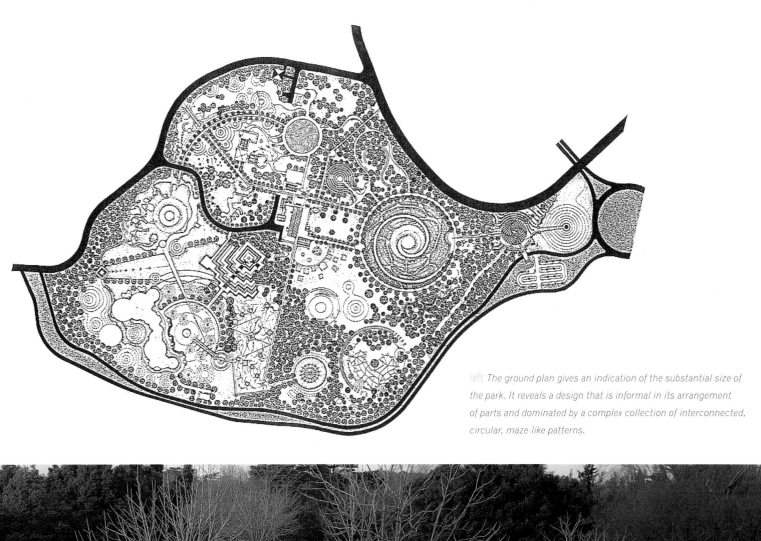

left The ground plan gives an indication of the substantial size of the park. It reveals a design that is informal in its arrangement of parts and dominated by a complex collection of interconnected, circular, maze-like patterns.

left *Pearlescent tiles are set densely on the inner surfaces of the concrete shelter where children play hide and seek. As well as displaying an infinity of colours, they are pleasantly smooth to the touch and give intriguing depth to the recesses in the walls.*

left *A primitive concrete shelter makes a play area calculated to stimulate the imagination. It suggests a cave or perhaps, with its pebble-encrusted feet and rounded contours, some kind of prehistoric animal.*

reform in Britain was much debated during this period, but it was some time before Loudon could put his ideas into practice. The first major public park, as opposed to an arboretum or a botanical garden, was designed in 1843 by Joseph Paxton at Birkenhead, Liverpool, and, setting the style of parks to come, it included lakes, paths, and rock gardens. By separating strollers from road traffic it provided them with a temporary escape from the surrounding urban environment. The only other significant development in the design of public parks occurred when they were included as an integral part of a city plan. The most notable example was the replanning of Paris, undertaken during the nineteenth century by Haussmann, who saw the establishment of a network of public spaces as essential to the development of cities in general.

By the end of the 1860s most major cities in Britain and France had public parks and this inspired other European countries and the Americas to follow suit. The first Western-style public park in Japan was Hibiya Park in Tokyo, which was opened in 1903. Subsequently, most parts of the developed world saw an expansion in the number of zoological parks and, in more recent decades, the birth of the theme park. In fact the modern evolution of the public park is probably best represented by the theme parks, such as Disneyland, which provide entertainment and recreation for old and young alike.

In Europe, and Britain in particular, since the 1950s the conventional urban park has been valued above all for its planting and floral displays. In Showa Memorial Park, horticulture is subordinated to the principal purpose of the park, which is to serve as a place for recreation for children. This design philosophy, which treats horticulture less reverentially than Western garden designers do, is in keeping with the traditional Japanese approach to the garden. The cultivation of shrubs and trees for its own sake is regarded as less important. Japan's garden culture is one in which trees may be shaped into idealized sculptural forms, and is based on broader aesthetic considerations and the value of symbolism rather than on the growing of plants for display. In Showa Memorial Park it is doubtless this attitude that has permitted the use of planting, and of trees in particular, to define and enclose individual landscape features rather than to create them. Here the garden is interpreted as a landscape for play and intellectual stimulation, not as a place for growing plants.

The overall plan of the park reveals an informal arrangement of parts, most of which are circular and linked by straight or curving paths defined by avenues of trees. The most impressive aspect is the sheer scale of the landscaping. The circular, patterned play area illustrated here, although large, represents only a fraction of the area of the landscaped park. The recurring landscaping theme

above The layout of one of the more unusual play areas is best appreciated by being looked down on from a terrace. This landscape of truncated pyramids has at its centre a sunken fog garden, or "foggy forest," conceived by Fujiko Nakaya. Here a machine throws out clouds of mist that envelop what is in effect a huge environmental sculpture.

explores the ancient idea of the labyrinth or maze. There were labyrinths in gardens in ancient Egypt and they were a common feature in European garden design during the sixteenth and seventeenth centuries. A labyrinth is usually defined as a confusing arrangement of paths which, in some instances, takes the form of a puzzle. It is the element of puzzle that is explored in this park.

The designer Fumiaki Takano aimed to provide a number of different and stimulating recreation spaces for both children and adults. The extensive site consists of more than twenty unconventional environments. Surrounded by dense tree planting, these are all interconnected by a complex matrix of paths. Each space is designed to encourage a different response from the children (and their parents), and to provide different forms of activity, some intellectual, some physical. Many of the areas are

simply flat, circular arenas in which the ground is covered with labyrinths or similar complicated geometric patterns. Some are littered with objects, deployed like pieces of a board game; one includes an ornamental clock, perhaps to act as a time-keeper.

Other play areas are more three-dimensional. In one, organic sculptured forms made from concrete, their inner surfaces clad in bright metallic gems, provide an ideal environment for games of hide and seek. Portholes and tunnels add to the interest of these cavernous spaces. This creation recalls the architectural forms that Gaudí used to such spectacular effect in Barcelona's Parque Güell.

Some of the landscaped spaces look more like environmental sculptures than a conventional playground. One space, consisting of a large, square well and numerous square mounds, includes a machine that generates clouds of mist to produce a fog garden —

created by the artist Fujiko Nakaya – where children can run about or take refuge from the fray on the raised mounds.

Other spaces invite forms of play that are even more physically demanding. Especially challenging is one where brightly coloured netting is stretched in an eccentric manner between coloured steel posts to form a gigantic trampoline. Unlike many of the other play spaces, this one is modern in appearance, its detail clearly inspired by High Tech architectural structures, in particular the advances in roofing technology. It is very reminiscent of the German Pavilion designed by Frei Otto and Rolf Gutbrod for Expo 67 in Montreal, where a supporting net fixed to vertical masts was covered with a huge waterproof membrane.

The play aspect of the park is not simply a collection of equipment dotted about a landscape as in many playgrounds.

Instead the whole park has been shaped to the idea of play and recreation, and contoured and patterned accordingly. Architectural forms emerge, some organic, others more structural. A number of the maze-like patterns may hint at an ancient tradition, but their shapes are more contemporary in their graphic imagery. This landscape belongs unmistakably to a world of computer-generated patterns, science fiction, and high technology.

Showa Memorial Park has a wide range of designed elements, some of which hint at the traditional Oriental obsession with complex board games. Others, such as the steel-and-mesh adventure playground, are contemporary in design yet respect the fact that, while children are becoming ever more technologically adept, they still enjoy developing physical prowess. The park provides an environment that understands what children want.

above Brilliantly coloured nets, stretched at wild angles over equally eye-catching steel posts, create a High Tech environment for physically challenging activity. Primary colours divide the netting into sections, which collectively form an extensive play area.

ROW HOUSING

SCHAUDT aRCHITEKTEN

When a garden design is discussed the subject is normally a plot attached to a single dwelling. In this instance a team of enlightened architects has employed a High Tech approach in its design for a row of terraced houses in which the indoor and outdoor living spaces have been integrated.

Schaudt Architekten's innovative scheme is in Jungerhalde, a relatively wealthy suburb of the German city of Konstanz, where large, detached houses predominate. Wishing to bring a greater social mix to the district, the city authorities held a competition to encourage the development of contemporary-style, low-cost row housing. Most people associate row, or terraced, housing with the working-class dwellings that emerged in response to the Industrial Revolution in Britain. To accommodate a fast-growing workforce two-storeyed terraced houses were built, row upon row, near factories. In order to maximize their number, none had a garden, only a small backyard, and so the whole environment was devoid of greenery. Even in the terraced housing of the later twentieth century built in the new towns of Britain and northern Europe, which had shared landscaped areas to the front, the space at the rear was no more than a green backyard.

But in fact the terraced house had also provided accommodation for the middle classes since the late eighteenth century, as the demand for housing grew in fast-developing towns and cities. In Britain, as elsewhere in Europe, the economics of making the most of space led to the erection of substantial three- and four-storeyed properties. This style of housing continued to be built until around the start of the First World War. The Royal Crescent at Bath, in England, designed by John Nash, exemplifies the beginning of this more elegant type of row housing for the new middle class. Facing a large communal park or lawn, each identical property had a private garden to the rear, although these were rarely developed at the time into any form of ornamental garden. A similar development occurred in Europe and the USA. In all cases the garden was an afterthought.

Jungerhalde's row housing is a modern version of the older three-storeyed terraced house, but differs in that the outside is considered as much as the inside, and the back of each house is as important as the front. The interior space has been extended outdoors, thanks to the flexibility provided by the methods and materials employed. This development is defined as High Tech in that it makes use of as-found industrial components. Apart from the dividing walls and concrete cellars, the houses are made from galvanized-steel girders bolted together and braced by diagonal ties. The floors are oiled and waxed larch planks fixed to the girders. The bolt-together steel building system, which does not rely on heavy brick walls, has resulted in an open style of architecture. The glass curtain walls contribute further to the sense of space. In the rear elevation the steel structure allows the building to extend into and contribute to the garden space.

The layout of each dwelling is that of a conventional European three-storeyed terraced house. The living room is on the first floor, the master bedroom is on the top floor, and the dining room, kitchen and children's room are on the ground floor. However, a number of personal external spaces are also incorporated into the design. The second floor of each property has its own small private terrace recessed between each house. Further exterior spaces are provided through various forms of balconies and decks right down to the garden level.

right *The High Tech styling of the houses is exemplified by the glass and steel walls, the corrugated galvanized-iron roofs that extend beyond them to provide shade to the decks and outside living spaces, and by the industrial-style steps with railings.*

On the north side of each house is the main access area, including forecourt and carport. A perforated-steel walkway leads from the front door to this paved area, passing over stones and pebbles and between clumps of bamboo. There is an interesting contrast in texture and form between the rectilinear form of the walkway and the rounded forms of the stones below it. Raising the steel walkway above the small front garden, rather than setting it at ground level, where it would divide and diminish the garden like a conventional path, is a simple but effective device.

On the south side of the building a decked balcony at first-floor level extends the living room into the outside space. Above this upper deck a steel grille, fixed to two steel tubes suspended by stainless-steel cables, provides this sitting and dining area with shade. The corrugated-steel roofs extend over this elevation to provide further shade. At garden level there is an additional deck that serves the ground-floor accommodation. This adjoins a grassy area, intended for recreation and play, which merges into wilder, indigenous planting that drops down to a lake.

Here an architectural style has been devised that combines indoor and outdoor living space and provides garden space rather than turning its back on it. The use of machine-made elements demonstrates the designers' belief that high tech Modernist architecture can serve the needs of both house and garden, rather than being confined to commercial or institutional roles.

left The living room on the first floor is extended above the garden by a decked balcony. Shade is provided by a grille made from industrial steel supported by steel tubes which are suspended from above. The balcony provides an ideal place for outdoor eating or simply relaxing. Below it, another deck links the ground floor with the soft landscaping of the garden.

right In this vertical view down to the main entrance of one of the houses, a steel walkway leads from the door over an area of pebbles and rocks to a carport and forecourt area. Using only three elements – stones, a steel grille, and bamboo plants – the architects have created a front garden that is simple and requires little maintenance.

A REFLECTIVE GARDEN

mICHAEL bALSTON

This is a garden that is literally reflective in terms of its materials and figuratively so in that it mirrors the past. Michael Balston's essay in combining traditionally inspired planting with High Tech architectural forms respects gardening history and heralds the future, to produce a garden of striking contrasts.

Viewed from one side, this garden appears conventional. A richly planted mix of perennials and shrubs, and of foliage and flower, is fronted by a stepped lawn. The clearly defined geometry is the only apparent concession to Modernism. Look to the rear and the north-facing boundary, however, and the contrast could not be greater. Here the old is challenged by the new: hard-edged modern engineering confronts the lush, soft, and textural planting opposite it.

A horseshoe-shaped, stainless-steel wall surrounds the elliptical terrace at the back of the garden. This sitting area is covered by a leaf-shaped canopy stretched over a funnel of curved steel ribs. The floor is made of slabs of stone which are reassuringly solid and firm, in contrast to the tent-like framework above. A long channel of water is spanned dramatically by a High Tech architectural structure of tubular steel and wire, supporting sail-like shapes of synthetic canvas. Often used by architects, this fabric is weather-proof and ideal for gardens, providing both shelter and shade. Like huge steel palms, these man-made trees cast theatrical and ever-changing shadows over the garden. The fabric is semi-opaque and on its surface can be seen further patterns of light and shade created by the foliage of surrounding trees. The shadowy shapes change as the sun moves across the sky or the wind sways the trees.

The lawn, so much a feature of a conventional garden, also plays a part in this unorthodox design, where its function is almost ornamental. With its steps and its narrowness it suggests a means of access for maintenance of the borders, but as a route through the garden it is secondary to the covered boardwalk. If it had been intended to be a path, gravel would have been a more

below *Sails stretched over steel masts and high-tensile wire create areas of light and shade on the surrounding terrace, walkway, and planting. Additional shadows from adjacent established trees form further patterns on the canopies. Providing a contrast to this high tech pergola is a traditional English border containing a mixture of wild flowers, perennials, and shrubs.*

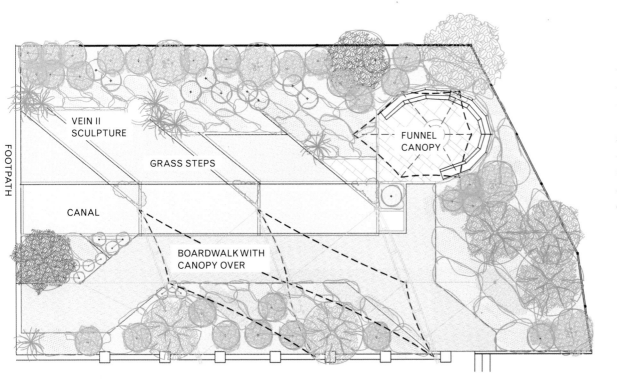

VEIN II
SCULPTURE

GRASS STEPS

FOOTPATH

CANAL

FUNNEL
CANOPY

BOARDWALK WITH
CANOPY OVER

left *This plan reveals a design based on strong diagonal lines. Although it is geometric, it is not formal or symmetrical. The canal that divides the garden in two for most of its length serves to separate the traditional lawn and mixed border from the modern canopied boardwalk.*

left *Steel planters are used instead of containers made of more conventional terracotta or stone. Their precise tubular shape and sharply defined apertures are a perfect foil for the lush, soft foliage of the hostas.*

right *Curving stainless-steel tubes arch upwards and outwards from a central point to support a tent-like canopy of synthetic canvas. This High Tech structure provides attractive height as well as shelter for a terrace walled in stainless steel. Stone paving is a link with the past and offers a textural contrast. The rough surface of the slabs sets off the polished steel that surrounds it.*

practical solution, but this would not have performed the visual role required. It is the presence of the reassuringly passive lawn that creates a transition from the soft verge of the planting to the hard edge of the canal and the structures that emerge from it.

A sculpture continues the theme of the contrast between old and new. *Vein II*, which stands between the lawn and the border, is a tall, obelisk-like piece that incorporates several pieces of weathered stone. At its base are reclaimed fragments of architectural elements, while at the top is a more decorative carved fragment. These historical artefacts are separated by an unashamedly modern column of glittering glass.

This garden of contrasts – of shadow and light, of old and new – proves that the introduction of new materials need not call for a new repertoire of plants. The long border, with its generous amounts of rhododendrons, foxgloves, delphiniums, and geraniums, is very traditionally English in content, while the arching, stem-like steelwork that overlooks it is international in architectural style. Yet they complement each other perfectly.

Balston's architectural features provide a radical alternative to the usual historical range of garden structures. Restricted to trellises, pergolas, and arbours, the latter were most often made of wood, sometimes combined with brick or stone, because all

these materials were deemed to be the most appropriate for use in the natural setting of a garden. Cast iron and steel had previously found favour only for the construction of greenhouses and conservatories, where the advantages of prefabrication or durability were essential. When iron and steel were employed in the garden, usually as gates or screens, they were used as decorative rather than structural mediums. For example, in the screens that enclose the Privy Garden at Hampton Court, London, designed by Jean Tijou towards the end of the seventeenth century, the iron was shaped into heraldic motifs and swirling floral patterns. Even the twentieth-century garden designer John Brookes and the Dutch landscape architect Preben Jacobsen were still relying on timber well into the 1970s, although in a simple, angular, and restrained manner, to provide structures within their essentially Modernist gardens.

It has long been common practice to clothe garden architecture and structures in greenery, normally using their frameworks as a support for climbing plants. In this garden the steel and wire are conspicuously free of any organic matter. By providing shade they may act like trees, but of course they are not intended to become them and, unlike conventional trees, once they are installed their effect is instant. One of the advantages of the new materials

left *An antique sculptured head, lying snugly on a carpet of hostas, spouts a gentle stream of water. While the fountain conjures up ancient Italianate gardens, the tubular steel poles and stainless-steel railings that surround it are very much of the present. It is a Romantic detail that works well in a Modernist context.*

being introduced into gardens is that while they provide strength they are also lightweight and slender. Although Balston's structure is large and covers a substantial part of the garden, it has none of the bulk and dominance that one would expect with a timber-and stone-construction of a similar scale. Despite its size it does not overwhelm the delicacy of the planting that faces it. Moreover, tubular stainless steel can be easily shaped, and here it provides elegant curvilinear forms that echo the surrounding trees. The material's mirror-like surface seems almost to dissolve in reflections of light and colour.

Traditional garden structures in wood, stone, or brick are expected to look their best after many seasons, when they have weathered, discoloured, and even deteriorated slightly. In this garden the structures are seen at their best from the start, although they will require maintenance in order to remain as they are intended to be seen. The canvas canopies will become soiled by leaves and by rain, dust, and the grime of an urban

environment. Traditional materials represent the aesthetics of the rustic and the homespun, whereas the new materials employed in this garden reflect the world of modern technology.

The planted border might be a link with the past, but the High Tech canopy and sails set the garden firmly in the twenty-first century. Just as High Tech architecture rejected the use of more seemingly long-lasting materials, such as brick or stone, in favour of more transitory ones, such as glass and plastic, so this garden challenges the concept of a garden as a place where both it and its users grow old gracefully. The success of this garden at the Chelsea Flower Show in 1999, where it won the award for the best garden of the event, indicates that it impressed a team of judges who, while renowned for their horticultural expertise, usually take a conservative, traditionalist outlook when it comes to assessing design. The positive reaction of the judges to this innovative garden underlines the growing notion that High Tech and horticulture need not be mutually exclusive.

THE PLASTIC GARDEN

dEAN CARDASIS

Sheets of coloured Plexiglas, a material more often encountered in High Tech architecture and interior design, were used to construct an unlikely yet perfectly appropriate central feature for the garden of an unusual suburban house situated near Northampton, Massachusetts.

below Plexiglas screens in bright colours, supported by a timber frame, extend into the garden from the French windows of the house. Dean Cardasis used this durable material to construct an imaginative device that connects house and garden.

The house, its exterior walls covered with vinyl, stands on a small plot in a row of dwellings set back from the road. To create gardens a strip of forest was cleared to a uniform depth behind the houses. This left a corridor of open space with no natural barriers between the houses to provide privacy. The owners of the house enlisted the help of garden designer Dean Cardasis. His objectives were to establish a sense of privacy, create a children's recreation area, and connect the house to the woodland behind it. His solution to this last problem was to bring house and woodland together by planting trees as close to the house as possible, effectively re-establishing the forest around the garden.

The positioning of the new trees was linked to a reshaping of the existing woodland, and the two processes produced three irregular, descending terraces. The largest of these was left as a lawn for the children to play on, another was gravelled and edged with stone, and the smallest, nearest the house and separating the other two, was floored with decking. The three terraces were further defined by a planting scheme of both native and indigenous species that served to extend the existing woodland. The result was an attractive and extremely low-maintenance garden.

Although the garden was now linked to the natural landscape, it still needed to be united with the house. The arrangement is informal and in plan its shapes bears little relationship to the rectangular outline of the house. His clients' house, Cardasis said, "was conceived with no regard to its site, and sat upon the opened woodland like an abandoned plastic toy." The incongruity between the house and its setting needed to be resolved. Cardasis took an imaginative approach. He linked the garden to the house, literally and in terms of materials, by introducing into the decked terrace a material similar to that used to construct the walls of the house. He used Plexiglas to create the Plastic Garden.

On entering the garden through the French windows one encounters a number of coloured Plexiglas screens, some single and others overlapped, that surround the small-decked outdoor

right Looking through a section of the overlapping, coloured, translucent panels reveals a subtle image of shadows and silhouettes. The interplay of the surrounding trees and the Plexiglas screens creates patterns of colour and light that range from soothing to stimulating.

eating area. Fixed to a timber frame, the rectangular plastic panels stand about 2m (6½ft) high; others are used horizontally to form a partial roof. A further series of colourful Plexiglas screens extends along the perimeter of the adjacent gravel terrace.

Cardasis is an admirer of the late landscape architect James Rose. Born in 1910, Rose was one of the twentieth century's most influential yet little-known American garden designers. His search for a new style was strongly influenced by the work of the Constructivists and other abstract sculptors and painters. His garden designs were mainly for residential properties and few survive in their original state. Those that are known demonstrate a great awareness of space and an understanding of twentieth-century lifestyle that has been absent from much garden design of recent decades. Rose took a great interest in the effects of light, shadow, sound, and space. He said that he found it helpful to think of a garden as a "sculpture which is large enough and perforated enough to walk through." A walk-through sculpture is exactly what Cardasis has created here, but with the benefit of Plexiglas he has taken Rose's concept a step further.

The Plastic Garden is a sculpture of colour and light. Its playful, light-transforming panels extend out from the house and affect

the way the whole garden is seen. As one looks out through the panels, the appearance of the surrounding elements, including plants, trees, and even the sky, is altered. They seem to have changed colour or to have been silhouetted. The overhead coloured panels change a cloudy sky into a clear-blue one. Light passing through the vertical panels bathes the nearby plants and surfaces in projected colour. The grey gravel terrace becomes a sea of red, orange, and yellow. As the sun moves, so do the coloured patterns. Viewed from certain angles, the Plexiglas also acts like a mirror, capturing images of trees or the sky.

The construction of *The Plastic Garden* is simple. Plexiglas is the modern stained glass, but it is stronger and lighter than glass. It is also much easier and safer to work with, although in fact many of the panels could be used as supplied. The frames that hold them were made from inexpensive, rough-cut timber and were also easy to assemble.

Cardasis restored and extended a woodland garden and then, through his innovative use of a man-made material that interacts with its natural surroundings, united it with the plastic house. A space that he described as bland, utilitarian, and spiritless has been transformed into a unified and characterful garden.

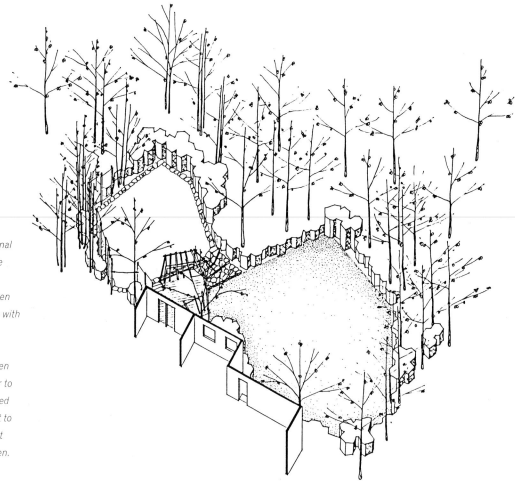

right *The three-dimensional drawing shows the simple layout of the garden. The existing woodland has been extended up to the house with new planting. Within this woodland three irregular stepped terraces have been formed. One is given over to lawn, another is a gravelled area. Between them, next to the house, is the smallest terrace, the Plastic Garden.*

above *Sheets of coloured Plexiglas are fixed horizontally to timbers to form a partial roof over the decked terrace of the Plastic Garden. When one looks up through them, the clouds and the branches of the overhanging trees are transformed into abstract patterns of a single colour.*

right *Sunlight shining through overlapping panels of red, orange, and yellow Plexiglas brings colour to the grey of the gravel garden and "paints" the foliage of nearby shrubs.*

THE KINETIC GARDEN

THE KINETIC GARDEN

One of the major changes that occurred in Western art at the beginning of the twentieth century was the rejection of the imitation of nature. In a change of direction pioneered by the Cubists and refined by the Constructivists, painting and sculpture embraced Abstraction. Movement had previously been merely represented in paint, clay, or stone, but now, in what was called kinetic art, it became real and a form of artistic expression. In 1920 Naum Gabo made what was probably the first kinetic sculpture. By electrically vibrating a wire so that it appeared to become a cone, he combined movement and illusion to create a temporary sculptural form. A few years later László Moholy-Nagy took kinetic art further with his *Light-Space Modulator*, a 2m (6½ft) high motorized construction of chrome-plated perforated steel, wire mesh, and glass. When this was set in motion in a darkened room and light was projected onto its varied moving surfaces, the light it reflected produced constantly changing shadows on the walls. But probably the best-known exponent of kinetic art is Alexander Calder, whose "mobiles" use only natural currents of air to create an entertaining aerial ballet of shape and colour. The painting equivalent of kinetic art was Op (or Optical)

left This 1960s advertisement for a new, man-made fabric reflects the influence of Op Art on design. The painting style attempted to suggest movement through optical illusion. Bridget Riley, its best-known practitioner, relied on the use of black and white stripes and her style is echoed here.

below The wavy, repeating pattern of this fabric, designed by Barbara Brown in 1960, preceded Op Art by several years but it nevertheless has the strong suggestion of movement which is characteristic of that style. This illusion is reinforced by the many bands of colour which constitute the wave shape and which are arranged in tonal order, progressing from dark to light.

Art, in which painters animated the surface of their canvases with disturbing optical tricks. The wavy, mainly black and white, optical patterns created by the British artist Bridget Riley even contributed, in the 1960s, to the adoption of the Op style by popular culture.

Unlike a painted canvas or a stone carving, a garden is never still, thanks to nature. But for centuries the creators of gardens have endeavoured to add more movement in order to entertain or simply for visual effect. They were perhaps the first kinetic artists and the kinetic addition they most often used was the fountain or another water feature. In Roman times advances in hydraulic engineering led to the development of ambitious fountains and there are descriptions of the sculptured fountains, splashing jets, and showy mosaic water features that graced ill-fated Pompeii.

With the revival of the classical villa in the late fifteenth century the fountain was the ideal creative vehicle for the sculptors of the day. Full of imagery and suggestion, it became the most important feature of a garden. In France and Italy the central columnar shafts were sculpted with mythological figures and water poured from a variety of orifices. By the seventeenth century the Italian sculptor Gianlorenzo Bernini had added a theatrical dimension. He was also a stage designer and this skill is evident in the fountain he created for the Piazza Navona in Rome. Less symmetrical and far less formal than previous free-standing fountains, it features a central giant obelisk, perilously supported over a hollowed-out rock, around which four gigantic figures symbolizing the four great rivers of the world (the Danube, the Nile, the Ganges, and the Plate) spout great jets of water.

Inventiveness in the use of water was not restricted to fountains. As long ago as the thirteenth century the creators of gardens developed devices known as automata which were able to provide all kinds of kinetic trickery, including sound. The history of gardens is full of mechanical devices that provided theatrical effects. Created during the Italian Mannerist era of around 1520 to 1600, the Villa d'Este at Tivoli had one of the most impressive collections of waterworks ever seen. The waters of a nearby river were diverted to serve the garden, which dropped from the villa in a series of terraces. There were fish ponds at the bases of the terraces, water staircases on either side of the main steps, the Promenade of a Hundred Fountains, and several self-contained multi-level fountains, none more spectacular than the Organ Fountain, which made water-powered "music." Water was used to build up air pressure in a rounded vault, which in turn caused an organ to play a repeating tune. Variation was provided by the power of another stream, which turned a toothed wheel whose

below Wind and water set these kinetic sculptures in motion. Designed by Alexander Calder, the colourful shapes bring movement and interest to a formal pool as they constantly change position.

teeth struck a keyboard which could imitate various sounds, including the trumpet and birdsong. The fountains also produced mist effects, which, when bathed in sunlight, gave rise to artificial rainbows. The automata no longer work, but the Villa d'Este remains one of the greatest kinetic gardens ever created. Trees and evergreen shrubs prevent its features from being seen collectively, so that there is an element of surprise as each is revealed.

Apart from the usual fountain or water feature, the modern era has seen little of the invention of previous centuries. Most spectacular water features, many designed by sculptors, have been confined to public parks or corporate buildings. While modern artists and sculptors have explored movement as an art form, using light machines, mobiles, and mechanical contraptions, kinetic effects have seldom been employed in the garden. In recent years, however, garden designers have discovered that many of their clients rarely see their gardens in daylight because they work long hours. Just as many of us now welcome twenty-

four-hour shopping, so there has developed a need for the "all-night" garden. This has been achieved mainly by the imaginative use of lighting, which itself has prompted the introduction of other theatrical effects, and today it is not unusual to find mist machines and outdoor sound systems in a garden. Lighting is not, strictly speaking, a kinetic feature, but as an agent that can radically change the appearance of a garden it is included here. And as garden designers have explored the potential of lighting and introduced more animated and performance-related lighting devices, the word "kinetic" has become more appropriate to describe this new design element.

It is not just at night that a garden can benefit from kinetic inventions, as the creators of the gardens of the past demonstrated. Today's kinetic technology makes all kinds of effects available to designers who want to increase the sensory pleasures of the garden. Some have even exploited the need to water a garden by turning an irrigation system into a kinetic sculpture.

above A water feature with a difference, this installation by the American landscape architect and artist Martha Schwartz makes use of irrigation devices to provide interest in a large site. They stand in orderly rows like trees in a newly planted orchard. With their tall "trunks" topped by sprinklers, they echo the forms of the nearby palm trees.

AN IDEA

lILIANA mOLTA & jEAN-CHRISTOPHE dENISE

In this kinetic garden both movement and sound are provided by a water feature. This is not in itself unusual, but this garden, shown in 1999 at a major international garden festival in France, uses fountains as an elaborate and sculptural irrigation system. Unlike conventional fountains, which play a purely aesthetic role, those of *An Idea* water and maintain the surrounding planting.

Occasionally a garden design appears to challenge the very concept of the garden, and the creation shown by Liliana Molta and Jean-Christophe Denise at Chaumont-sur-Loire in 1999 did just that. The park at the Château de Chaumont-sur-Loire has hosted the Festival International des Jardins since 1992 and each year designers and artists from around the world are invited to create gardens for it. The emphasis is on experimentation and innovation, but all designs must also be practicable.

An Idea consists of columns of upturned multicoloured plastic bottles impaled on iron rods used to reinforce concrete, which stand amid a sea of planting. There are so many of these colourful plastic columns that they dominate the whole space. The numerous varieties of polygonum – the only genus of plant employed in this scheme – from which the columns emerge include both ornamental and even edible types. Apart from paths that provide access and define the planting areas, the polygonums and their eye-catching watering devices constitute the whole garden.

In plan the layout of the garden seems to be almost conventional and inspired by the past. The design is formal and symmetrical, with paths that lead to and divide the area into precisely defined planting beds and borders. In content, however, it is thoroughly modern, a garden equivalent of the eccentric automated sculptures of the Swiss artist Jean Tinguely, whose electrically driven machines and mechanical artworks clatter and bang as they fulfil some programmed task. Tinguely's sculptures, characterized by their built-in malfunctions and unmechanical waywardness, consist of a chaotic collection of cogs, wheels, drive belts, and electric motors that work together to make abstract paintings, play "catch ball" with children, and even self-destruct. Most akin to *An Idea* is his garden "fountain," in which a rubber hosepipe is bent and erratically waved about by a machine, soaking unwitting passers-by.

The use of disposable found objects in a repetitious manner is Minimalist in spirit and this approach is reinforced by the decision to employ only one genus of plant. Visually, however, the planting is far from Minimal, as there is great diversity between the species. Few other genera of plants display such variation in size and habit. *Polygonum polystachyum*, which can reach 1.8m (6ft) in height, produces fragrant flowers in the autumn, whereas *Polygonum bistorta* is smaller and clump-forming and displays pale-pink, bottlebrush flowers in late spring. Furthermore the

right As far as the eye can see, upturned plastic water bottles of various colours are stacked in columns to provide an irrigation system that suggests an art gallery rather than a garden. Water rises and falls in the columns, the resulting gurgling noises adding to the entertainment.

left This beautiful tinted drawing reveals a design that appears both formal and conventional. Only on closer inspection does one see the forest of slender columns that transforms the garden into an environmental artwork.

leaves are edible and can be added to salads. *Polygonum affine* "Darjeeling Red" is an energetic ground-cover plant, with a long flowering season and the bonus of foliage and dried flower heads that provide autumn colour.

Polygonums in general prefer a moist soil and therefore it was necessary to calculate how much water would be required each week to sustain the plants during the hot and dry French summer. Here technical expertise was provided by Jean-Christophe Denise, who is an architect. Molta and Denise worked out that 20 litres (5¼ US gallons) of water would be required to irrigate one square metre (10¾ sq ft) of planting. In terms of plastic bottles this translated into two columns, each 1.5m (5ft) high. Calculations also took into consideration the fact that some species require more water than others.

Water bubbles up from the base to the top of the stacks of interpenetrating upturned bottles, filling each bottle in succession until each column becomes a miniature reservoir. On reaching the top the water gushes over, briefly irrigating the surrounding plants before draining away from the column, with much gurgling, until the device is empty. Then the cycle is repeated. Unlike the anarchic sculptures of Tinguely, many of which exist merely to destroy themselves, the function of this garden is to care for and perpetuate itself.

As its name suggests, *An Idea* is a conceptual garden. Molta has worked on projects in cinema, fashion, and architecture and so brought to it a wide experience in solving design problems. She was able to define the garden in her own terms as she is not solely a creator of gardens and is therefore less inhibited by the history of the discipline. Although this project dispenses with many of the ingredients that are customarily found in a conventional garden, such as lawns and mixed borders, it is still identifiable as a garden; although it contain only polygonums, it is still a place where plants are cultivated. The plastic columns might look like an environmental artwork but their purpose is to provide irrigation. *An Idea* is certainly unorthodox, but it is nevertheless a garden dedicated to growing plants, where an imaginative sculptural watering system provides a fascinating and efficient alternative to the hose and sprinkler.

right A single clear irrigation column emerges from a mass of polygonums. Ornamental and edible varieties of this genus are the only planting used in this garden. The unusual construction of the column, in which inverted plastic bottles are impaled on a concrete-reinforcing rod, is clearly visible.

PLAZA OF WHITENESS

SHUNMYO mASUNO

This landscaped plaza in Japan introduces real movement into a modern Zen garden. Water features are not normally present in the traditional Zen garden, but this metaphorical landscape is not the familiar one of stone and raked gravel. It is a garden in which change over time is not just incidental but is central to the spiritual message conveyed by the design.

Shunmyo Masuno designed the plaza for the National Research Institute for Metals, Science and Technology in Tsukuba City. Enclosed by the Institute's buildings and with a restaurant in one corner, the plaza could have been simply a place where the scientists met socially. But Masuno's landscaping was intended to offer more than this. It was designed to provide a spiritually uplifting experience that is related to the work of the Institute.

Although trained as a landscape architect, Masuno is also a priest. In 1979 he entered the Daihonzan-Soji-ji temple, where he underwent ascetic training before becoming assistant resident priest at the Kenkoh-Ji temple. This experience might begin to explain his approach to this site.

Appropriately for a metals research establishment, Masuno's design was inspired by man's quest for a precious metal. His idea recollects the American Gold Rush, when prospectors sought their fortunes in the mountains of the USA and Canada. That dry and barren environment is what he has imitated here. In their search for water, gold-seekers would meet at springs and waterholes, but most of the time they worked alone, digging and panning for ore. Like the prospectors, the researchers employed by the Institute tend to work independently. For them the plaza is the equivalent of the spring, a meeting place where feelings of isolation and solitude can be shared and relieved.

The idea that emerged for the plaza was of a collection of stones scattered about a chalky landscape. Granite boulders from Hiroshima Prefecture and Aji stones from Kagawa were chosen and positioned with care and understanding, in the way of the ancient Zen gardeners; their arrangement was guided by Masuno's

many drawings and studies. The garden is a modern variation on the traditional Zen garden, but here the large, layered rocks do not evoke a Japanese landscape but are a metaphor for individual human lives. Each rock is described by the designer as "strong and sharp," and their alignment – they all point towards the buildings – represents the researchers' spirit and determination.

The underlying theme of the garden is purity. The stones, washed by rain and blasted by the wind, are seen as being gradually "purified." This process of change over a period of time provides an analogy for the purification of a man's spirit by the experience of harsh circumstances. White, a colour that dominates the scheme, is the symbol of purity in Buddhist culture. In Zen philosophy the power of nature revitalizes the worn-out mind and restores the purity of the spirit in the same way that stones are bleached by the sun. The scientists working at the Institute need pure and clear minds to carry out their work and the garden is intended, through its symbolic forms, to help them achieve this.

The site is rectangular, with the restaurant in the eastern corner. The area around that semicircular building is paved in a square geometrical pattern of Chinese granite interrupted by symbolic natural boulders of Korean granite. Opposite the restaurant one can leave the plaza via a wide promenade. Diagonally opposite, in the western corner, is a large, irregular triangle of grass. Bisecting this is a straight, stepping-stone-like path that spans a stony "river" by means of two simple stone-slab bridges. The loose stones represent a dry riverbed which has a low fountain as its source. The water emerges from a stone that gives the illusion of being a natural spring. The river of stones

Looking along the straight, stepping-stone path towards the restaurant, one is presented with a landscape inspired by the inhospitable terrain that prospectors encountered during the American Gold Rush of the mid-nineteenth century. A meandering path of stones suggests a dry riverbed, while the crazed paving in the foreground is reminiscent of baked, cracked earth.

weaves its way from the northern corner across the square within a surrounding area of crazed paving that loosely follows its course. This random patterning is reminiscent of the sun-baked surface of a dried-out pond or river. The stones of the dry river "flow" through the grass triangle but, as they enter it, the crazed-paving edge on one side branches off to suggest the remnants of a previous course of the river. The "river" continues past the restaurant, to culminate in a triangular bed of rocks, perhaps hinting at a delta. It is here that relief from the dry, harsh natural landscape recreated by Masuno is provided by a second water feature. This takes the form of a mist fountain which creates an effect similar to a thermal spring or, perhaps more appropriately, the heat haze in the desert, which can give rise to the frustrating illusions of water seen in mirages.

Movement and flow are suggested by a dry river, but this begins and culminates with real water features. Whereas the traditional Zen garden was a place of stillness and silence, this landscape is more lively and contains kinetic features. Fountains were not part of the formal Zen garden, although they occur in domestic Japanese gardens. The design of the plaza continues the Japanese interest in the landscape as an inspiration for gardens. Unusually, in this case the landscape is a distant one. In Japanese gardens, stones and gravels were often used to imitate water. Here they are used more literally to describe a waterless riverbed.

In its references to Zen, this garden represents the traditional spiritual aspects of Japanese culture. At the same time it is both contemporary and international in its interpretation of the natural landscape and its sophisticated water features.

above A mist fountain set within a precise triangle of stones provides kinetic interest in this modern interpretation of the traditional Japanese Zen garden. Within the theme that inspired the garden it also represents a place where the prospectors would refresh themselves. By implication, the researchers who work at the Institute can find spiritual refreshment there.

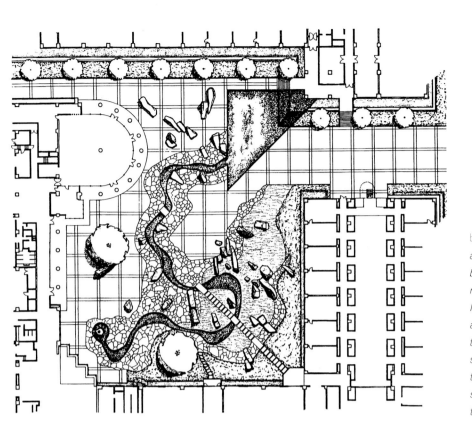

right *The plan drawing shows clearly the course of the dry "river" of stones as it rises from a spring in the northern corner of the plaza and weaves its way through a grassy area and past the restaurant to the rocky triangle that contains the mist fountain. The plaza is strewn with carefully placed groups of rocks, some of which are cut into the more formal granite paving.*

below *Large rocks, chosen and arranged with great care by the designer of the plaza, represent the lives of the Institute's staff. They are all aligned so that they focus on the research buildings that surround the plaza, and together they symbolize the spirit and determination of those who work there.*

A THEATRE OF LIGHT

JENNY JONES

Using glass, mirror-calm pools of water, and reflective surfaces, combined with a subtle exploitation of natural phenomena such as dew and condensation, the theatre designer Jenny Jones has created a garden for herself and her husband that presents an ever-changing performance of visual effects.

Situated at Garstons, a secluded eighteenth-century farmhouse, the garden is set on a windy escarpment on the Isle of Wight, off the south coast of England. Instead of relating the garden to the monotonous agricultural landscape of bare or cultivated fields that surrounds it, Jenny Jones chose to separate it from its environment. There was also a practical reason for enclosing the newly created garden – its planting needed protection from both the prevailing south-westerly winds and the local rabbit population. The result is a garden that functions like a sanctuary or refuge: an intimate space within an expansive landscape, with only a restricted view of the fields and sea beyond.

The garden is contained not by conventional walls but by a combination of glass and timber screens. Within these the design has evolved as a series of related and interconnected spaces which are essentially self-contained gardens. A degree of order is provided by a narrow boardwalk which divides the garden down its entire length. It spans the lower terrace garden next to the house and separates the upper gravel garden and pond garden. In the centre of the pond garden is the Pond House, accessible only via a wooden walkway from the lower garden between two mirror-like pond-retaining walls that are clad in black stainless steel. The building provides shelter and a place to entertain, but, being partly immersed in the pond, it achieves an intimacy with the garden that a conventional summer house could not provide. Inside, the silence is disturbed only by the rippling of water and rustling of grasses.

If you look across the water from the Pond House on a still day, a *Chamaerops humilis* can be seen reflected in the pool. Growing from a bed of gravel, this winter palm is protected by a glass

left *Seen from the sunken Pond House, a winter palm is perfectly mirrored in the motionless water. Behind the palm a clear pane of glass, which helps to protect the plant from cold winds, drips with condensation. Like a tableau, it is a scene of stillness, any movement almost imperceptible.*

above *The Pond House, with its truncated-pyramid roof, is the garden's only architectural feature. Surrounded by a deep moat and with its windows at water level, it offers an intimate view of the pond and the garden. Inside, one is as close to being outdoors as it is possible to be while enjoying protection from the elements.*

right *Jenny Jones's coloured isometric drawing, itself a work of art, explains the relationship of the various gardens and features within the whole project. Towards the bottom can be seen the terrace garden, The Water Harp, and the pathway leading to the entrance to the Pond House. Towards the top are the upper pond and the gravel garden with its large glass prism.*

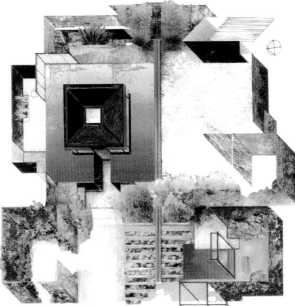

above *The silver plumb bobs of the Water Harp hang on stainless-steel wires just above the surface of a lily pond. Water, supplied through a pipe by a pump above, trickles down the wires to disturb the placid surface of the pond. The plumb bobs occasionally touch the water, which causes gentle ripples to radiate across it.*

screen, whose appearance is transformed when condensation forms on it, and a nearby brightly coloured wall. The arrangement of the elements is like a stage set which changes according to nature's cycle. Additional movement and sound are provided by grasses, the black *Ophiopogon planiscapus* 'Nigrescens' and the blond *Stipa tenuissima* in the nearby gravel garden.

Jenny Jones's background in the theatre has also encouraged her use of innovative materials. A sphere and ring of aluminium lie at the centre of the gravel garden, where black-glass walls reflect the silver trunks of *Betula utilis* var. *jacquemontii*. Near the pond is a "golden screen" of Dutch metal (paper-thin leaves of brass that are applied to surfaces and can be, as here, varnished). Narrow glass windows in the screen give a glimpse of the garden beyond.

One of the most daring features of this garden is a large prism constructed from three 2.4m (8ft) sheets of 10mm (½in) thick strengthened glass joined together by custom-made steel fixings. This structure houses the black bamboo *Phyllostachys nigra* and also acts as a piece of sculpture. The appearance of many of the

hard landscape materials used in the garden, particularly the glass of the prism, changes in response to the weather. Sometimes it conceals the bamboo inside. At other times it reflects the grasses in the gravel garden and the image of the distant house or a wonderfully confusing mixture of the bamboo and the surroundings. The glass also has a practical function in sheltering plants that are accustomed to warmer climates.

Another feature is both a visual and a kinetic attraction. The Water Harp is essentially a hardwood frame that traverses a pool in the lower garden. Water is pumped through a concealed hose into a stainless-steel tube supported by the frame. After exiting through small holes in the tube it trickles down stainless-steel wires held straight by silver plumb bobs. The gentle sound as the water dribbles down the wires can be appreciated from a nearby hardwood seat, similar in form to the Water Harp.

In this theatrical garden the mirrored surfaces of water and glass promote an interplay between the spectator's senses and the constantly changing light and weather.

*A glass prism sits on the edge of the gravel garden,
providing a geometric sculptural element. The metal sphere below
adds formal contrast. The appearance of the prism changes
throughout the day. Here early-morning dew drips down the glass,
slowly revealing the bamboo plants inside.*

TOUCHED BY WIND

mAKATO SEI WATANABE

Situated deep in the mountains of Gifu Prefecture in Japan, Mura-no Terrace, a new cultural and information complex, is a modern and technological response to a site surrounded by magnificent but daunting natural features.

Movement is the principal theme in this landscape scheme, designed by Makato Sei Watanabe. As modern as it seems, this site reflects the philosophy of generations of Japanese garden makers. Adjacent to one of the country's least populated villages, it is blessed with spectacular scenery. But in this remote area large-screen televisions illuminate the night. The local inhabitants enjoy what most Japanese city dwellers can only dream of: the comforts of urban life provided by advanced technology within unspoilt natural surroundings. Mura-no Terrace is unashamedly High Tech and was designed to serve as a venue for small concerts and festivals, as well as a meeting place for local people and an information centre for visitors.

Watanabe's landscaping is in the spirit of traditional Japanese gardens, which for centuries have paid homage to the wonders of nature. Any remarkable phenomenon, from a specimen tree to a

distinctively shaped rock, from a waterfall to a cliff, can command reverence. Similarly, at Mura-no Terrace, the idea was not to ignore nature or to alter it but to draw inspiration from it in a way that would emphasize and worship its beauty. The first aim was to help visitors to experience the landscape, in particular a sparkling river that flowed below the site. The answer was to build a dramatic viewing deck that is cantilevered so that it seems to fly out over the river. This feature looks down to the water and on to the mountains but does not intrude into the natural landscape. The chosen solution illustrates the fact that landscape design need not always involve changing the landscape to meet either aesthetic or functional requirements, but can simply provide access or views.

However, the building of the complex did necessitate some new landscaping, and the recurrent theme of this is movement, both suggested and real. Water is one of the basic elements of a

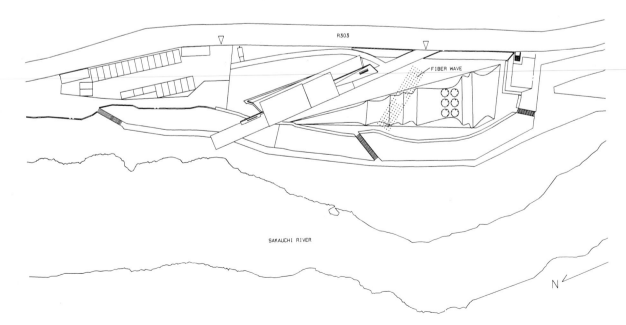

left At the bottom left of this plan of Mura-no Terrace can be seen the cantilevered deck that projects out from the complex. This suspends visitors above a river and provides a fine view of the mountains facing the site.

above *With its High Tech architectural surfaces reflecting the sky, the complex is set in a remote rural location that offered the designer the opportunity to try out a variety of futuristic landscape ideas. Embracing modern engineering and electronics, the sculptural features pay homage to the majesty of the surrounding landscape of mountains and rivers.*

Japanese garden. It need not always be real and in fact moving water is often only suggested by an inventive and observant use of stone or gravel. In keeping with this tradition, outside the building that faces the deck there is a landscape feature that appears to be a large, green wave. In *The Edge of Water,* as this creation is called, man-made landscaped forms integrate with and echo the natural landscape that surrounds the site. The concept is linked with a further tradition in Japanese gardens in which a miniature version of nature is arranged within a natural setting. The Minimalism of this green mound, the only planted area in the complex, is also typically Japanese. It is in the spirit of the rock and gravel Zen gardens of the fourteenth and fifteenth centuries, in which landscape was suggested by reducing it to its essential forms. As in these historical gardens, the flowing, sculptural forms at Mura-no Terrace are intended to promote contemplation as much as to produce a decorative effect, although in this case the mound is also functional, serving as a seating area for an audience when the deck is used as a stage.

Real movement in a traditional Japanese garden is usually provided by running water, in the form either of a stream or a waterfall. But there is a history of other kinetic devices, some bringing sound into gardens, such as the dripping of water from a bamboo flume, or pipe, into a water basin, the chiming of a wind bell, and, most famously, the sozu. Water enters from a flume into the diagonally cut end of the sozu. When the sozu is full the diagonal end drops and water flows out so that the other end returns to its former position, hitting a rock at its base and thus producing a loud, hollow sound.

In this garden real movement is provided by an environmental sculpture that both understands nature and reflects Japan's romance with state-of-the-art technology. *Touched by Wind* uses 150 4m (13ft) tall carbon-fibre rods to evoke a field of grass rippling like waves in the breeze or trees swaying and rustling in the wind. Watanabe was inspired by natural kinetic activity, noting that living things, even plants rooted to the ground, are never still. Their position, form, and shape change constantly in response to wind, rain, temperature, and light. They stand in such a way as to expend as little energy as possible, and it is from this survival mechanism that their beauty comes. Watanabe set out to create, in man-made form, an entity that had such "primal beauty."

Reproducing the mechanisms of a living organism by artificial means requires technologies such as carbon fibre, solar cells, and bright, light-emitting diodes. The carbon-fibre rods, equipped with solar batteries and luminous diodes on their tips, remain still unless stimulated. When the wind blows, however, they bend gently and sway. At night the luminous diodes, having been charged by sunlight during the day, start to blink with light as they sway, providing a light feature that is also kinetic. Most kinetic devices are primarily mechanical and repeat identical events, but the movement in this work is not mechanical but natural and is in harmony with the natural elements. The blue lights sway back and forth like fireflies. This is a free and relaxing movement, not under the control of the designer, and its shape is left to nature. The feature may be seen as a sculptural equivalent of plants and their behaviour. Technology is used here not to imitate nature but to highlight its phenomena.

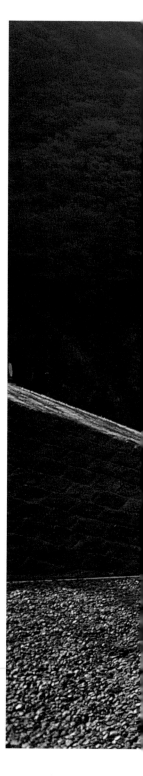

left The uncluttered deck is an ingenious landscape design device. It visually connects the architecture of the complex with the surrounding countryside without invading or otherwise detracting from its beauty and drama.

above *The slightest breeze will set the sea of carbon-fibre rods in the foreground swaying like tall grass in a gentle wind. In the background a wave-like green mound echoes the forms of the encircling tree-covered mountains.*

GARDEN AT TAKAPUNA

tED sMYTH

After darkness falls a narrow rear-courtyard garden is transformed into a colourful and enigmatic space by the lighting effects of the New Zealand garden designer Ted Smyth. He was formerly an artist whose paintings were inspired by rainbows. This fascination with the spectrum may explain his use of lighting that one might associate more with Las Vegas than with a quiet domestic garden.

Lighting and automatic watering systems are the most common forms in which modern technology has found its way into the garden. The necessity to include both in a garden reflects the demands of today's lifestyles. This is more likely to be so in urban societies, where long working hours and a wide choice of leisure activities result in little time being spent at home during the day. Many busy people want a garden that both looks after itself as much as possible and can be enjoyed even when it is dark. It must be as interesting by night as it is by day.

While lighting has become a commonplace feature of the garden, it consists in many cases mainly of a number of spotlights distributed around the space to illuminate particular plants, ornaments, and paths so that they are visible or accessible at night. Often the most ambitious addition to such a garden is a submersible light that highlights a fountain.

However, the increasing nocturnal demands on the garden have stimulated many of today's garden designers to see lighting as an integral design element rather than an afterthought. In doing so some have considered the garden as a stage set to be lit for an evening performance, and well-planned lighting can certainly lend it a theatrical look. Here Ted Smyth has created a light show that transforms the garden as daytime turns to dusk and then night falls. As the lighting begins to take effect, it changes the mood and complexion of the garden, adding a sense

right *A steel sculpture is bathed in stray light from nearby rooms. In the background the neon-lit portals wash everything within them with a blue light. The walls and trellis panels take on the appearance of large Minimalist paintings. These effects, combined with the reflections in the ornamental pool, transform the small courtyard into an almost theatrical experience at night.*

of mystery. Designers of such gardens have often employed lighting systems and technology that are far removed from the uplighters and downlighters of standard garden lighting. In the garden at Takapuna, Smyth has dispensed with conventional approaches and used a type of brash lighting more usually employed for utilitarian or commercial purposes: neon.

He has used neon lights to enliven a series of walled, confined spaces after dark. In some respects this courtyard garden is conventional. By day rocks, cobbled paving, trellis, white walls, and exotic and ground-cover planting prevail. The white-rendered concrete walls, topped by a strip of trellis, conceal the owners' tennis court beyond. Appropriately entitled *Trunks and Vines*, the contemporary tubular-steel sculpture that sits in the ornamental pool gives the garden a sense of modernity. But the most novel and intriguing feature is the large, plain, bulky, window-like portals that stand proud of the walls. Each is free-standing, detached from its neighbours, and stands as high as the

trellis-capped wall onto which it backs. By day these identical openings break up the long wall like a series of picture frames, each with its own three-dimensional "painting" of planting, rocks, and blue trellis. Within the portals that are opposite the ornamental pool a rectangular trellis panel is set into the wall, like another window, to give a glimpse of the tennis court.

It is as night falls that the portals reveal their primary purpose. They become a source of light as the discreet neon tubes that run the full length of their undersides begin to emit a blue glow. The light paints the wall, trellis, and planting within the portals mainly blue, although other colours are also evident. The appearance of everything within them is transformed. What is more, the boundaries of the courtyard, clearly defined and restricted by day, are now less clear. Stray light from rooms that overlook the space provides the only additional source of illumination. The lighting and the portals are minimal in concept and form, but they combine to create a dramatic nighttime garden.

The effect is similar to that of the neon sculptures made by the artist Dan Flavin in the late 1960s. His clusters of neon lights, sometimes suggesting shapes and at other times defining space, were seen as intended only when illuminated. Similarly the role of Smyth's "light portals" becomes clear only when night falls and they become windows of light.

Neon light has no single point of origin and therefore it creates none of the sharp shadows of conventional garden lights. Instead everything is bathed uniformly in an electrifying glow. It can also be hidden more easily than spotlights. Since they do not generate any heat, neon light sources can be safely covered and can be set in architectural structures, as in this garden. Neon even has a distinctive sound, a hum that is just audible.

In most domestic gardens lighting is simply intended to enhance what is already there. In this garden, however, it is itself a design feature, part architecture and part sculpture. Today's lighting technology offers the imaginative garden designer many opportunities. After seeing how Smyth has used neon in this garden, it is not difficult to imagine the effects that could be achieved by introducing other less common light sources, such as laser or fibre-optic lighting, into almost any outdoor space.

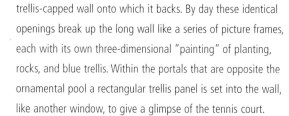

below *Even in daylight the neon lights have an intriguing effect. The portal glows blue, while within it trellis, rocks, and planting are framed as if in a three-dimensional painting. An illuminated white screen in the centre of the opening highlights a colourful feature plant.*

right *Bathed in cool blue light, the contrasting shapes of the agave and the spherical sculpture both take on a mysterious appearance. The strange effect is produced by the inventive use of neon tubes, in preference to conventional garden lighting. Unlike spotlights, neon light sources do not become hot and, as here, they can be discreetly concealed within an architectural feature.*

ARCHITECTURAL EXTENSIONS

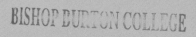

ARCHITECTURAL EXTENSIONS

In renewing the close acquaintance of architecture and the garden, the New Tech garden has revived an association that goes back to the Renaissance. In 1452 the Italian architect Leon Battista Alberti wrote that the house and garden should be treated as an integrated whole and that the garden should not be enclosed but be projected into the landscape. An elevated site was therefore deemed preferable. These principles were to shape the style of the Renaissance garden. The garden at the fifteenth-century Villa Cicogna Mozzoni at Bisuchio, with its architectural pools and sunken garden, illustrates perfectly Alberti's concept of

architecture extending into the garden and vice versa. Set on a hillside, the villa was laid out to exploit the changing levels and as a result each floor has access to a different garden. An impressive water staircase connects the formal garden with the surrounding woodland and meadows. With the garden of the Villa Belvedere in Rome the garden architect Donato Bramante went one step further. Here even the terrain is moulded into architectural forms, including a stage, terraces, staircases, and ramps.

In Europe this intimate association between house and garden was generally maintained by a continuing preference for

formalism. However, in eighteenth-century England the new
landscape movement instigated a less formal and more "natural"
approach to garden design. Architecture was given a more
detached role, providing elaborate bridges and follies in a
landscape where minimally maintained fields were allowed to
encroach on the walls of an elegant Palladian house. This concept
was given new life in the twentieth century by the Swiss-born
architect Le Corbusier, especially in those buildings that were raised
above the ground on stilts and where the surrounding meadows
continued up to the supports. With no terraces and no gardens,
the building was completely independent of its surroundings.

Not all architecture sought to be detached from its environment
or from the garden. Since the nineteenth century the most common

architectural way to link the house with the garden has been
the domestic conservatory. Originally made of wood, it became
popular in Victorian times as a glass-covered extension to the
dwelling. A true outdoor room, the conservatory provided a
protected environment for tender plants and for sensitive souls
who wished to enjoy the garden without catching a cold.

In the USA the use of glass predominated in the domestic
architecture of Richard Neutra during the 1940s and Mies van der
Rohe during the 1950s, in which space was no longer confined by
solid walls. Neutra's houses extended over their sites, simultaneously
defining gardens and framing views of the distant landscape.
Innovative building methods and methods, including steel and
glass construction, prefabrication, and new synthetic materials,

contributed to a more open and fluid architecture in which external and internal spaces interact and the garden is conceived as part of the house. Thus it was through architects and not garden designers that the building and the garden came to be linked once more. Covered walkways, aerial jetties, and roofless rooms are just a few of the devices that have been used in contemporary domestic architecture to extend the house into its environment.

Today architects such as Antoine Predock and Steven Ehrlich are contributing directly to the development of the garden. They have inspired garden designers to consider modern materials and methods as well as to develop a greater awareness of three-dimensional space. Many of their ideas have allowed gardens to be created in unlikely places, ranging from rooftops to treetops. A heightened understanding of thinking in three dimensions has led to multi-level gardens. Where ground space is costly or limited, why not build upwards? A small space in an urban environment is often a shaded and gloomy one, and here a vertical garden can provide the answer. The most impressive example of a vertical garden must be that created by the architects Enrique Browne and Borja Huidobro for an office block in Santiago, Chile. Here the relationship between garden and building is as intimate as it can be, for the external cladding to the stepped west elevation is a green curtain wall of planting.

below Dan Pearson's commission for the Millennium Dome in London required him to plant a series of stepped narrow terraces along tall walls that concealed unsightly services. The addition of lighting helps to enhance the effect of a vertical garden.

above The Gold-Friedman Residence, designed by Steven Ehrlich, uses colourful tiles and built-in sofas to create the feeling of an outdoor room. A steel bridge connects the house to an upper terrace and the adjoining hillside.

right For this office block in Santiago, Enrique Browne and Borja Huidobro created a hanging garden whose luxuriant planting is both a design feature and a means of screening the west side of the building from the sun.

GARDEN AND CONSERVATORY

STEPHEN WOODHAMS & PETER ROMANIUK

A London house is provided with both garden and conservatory through the use of materials and building methods more often associated with modern commercial architecture. Combined with adaptable planting in containers, this approach makes maximum use of the restricted urban space.

The traditional conservatory originated in England in Victorian times to make it possible to sit in the garden even when poor weather prevented it. This glass room attached to the house allowed its occupants to enjoy an expansive view of the garden and surrounding landscape. The conservatory is the simplest way in which the architecture of the house can be extended into the garden, and its addition rarely calls for significant alteration to the house. Originally it was made of wood and glass but more recently bricks have been used for the lower part. The modern conservatory is very often a pale imitation of the elegance and detail of its Victorian and Edwardian predecessors.

Many conservatories are built as extensions to large houses with large gardens. In this instance, however, the conservatory was to occupy a very small space and was intended to maximize the new covered area without visually compressing the minute garden. Also, because adjacent tall buildings dominated the garden, making it gloomy, it was important that the conservatory should create as little additional shade as possible.

With these considerations in mind the architect, Peter Romaniuk, decided early on that the walls, the roof, and even the supporting members were to be glass; only the door frames were to be made of another material – in this case metal. The development of glass has been so successful as a structural material that it is now employed in many ways in architecture. In a demonstration of its newly acquired strength, there are even instances of its being used for flooring bridges. The floor of the conservatory is also made of glass, in this case a fine-textured opaque variety. This is raised above the ground on steel girders, and beneath the glass there are lights which at night provide

the main source of illumination for the all-glass room. A clear-glass panel in the centre of the floor reveals a puzzling group of what seem to be dinosaur eggs nestling on a bed of carpet.

Because the conservatory is so open and transparent, the dividing line between the inside and the outside seems to evaporate. The garden, newly created as part of the project, is a continuation of the glass-enclosed structure. It is raised off the ground and is on two levels. The "floor" of the garden is made of Flow Form, a galvanized-steel grille made of parallel vertical strips held slightly apart by rods. Flow Form is normally used for industrial factory flooring or exterior fire escapes, but, despite these unglamorous associations, here it is used to great aesthetic effect. At night the garden can be illuminated by lights beneath the grille and planting can be encouraged to grow through it, as is intended here. The garden's other surfaces are all constructed from types of modern metal. Low, vertical retaining walls and additional surfaces have been created by the use of aluminium chequer plate. This non-slip, textured and patterned, flooring material has found favour in many situations, but its combination of lightness and durability makes it particularly suitable as a floor covering in the transport industry, where it receives heavy use.

The planters that sit on these surfaces are made from galvanized sheet steel, rolled and formed into various cylindrical or tapering forms. Their precise lines and shapes are designed to highlight the planting within. Permanent plantings of evergreen bamboos and phoenix palms are enhanced by the addition of seasonal displays and cut flowers in the same style of planter. Simple white hyacinths are complemented in the spring by paper-white narcissi, which are followed later in the season by white

right The conservatory and the garden space are linked by their similar use of High Tech materials. Different kinds of glass and various metallic surfaces are the only materials used. Inside the glass conservatory the elevated floor is made from toughened, opaque, acid-etched glass. Under a sheet of glass set into the floor there are four rows of objects that resemble huge eggs. Their significance is left to the imagination.

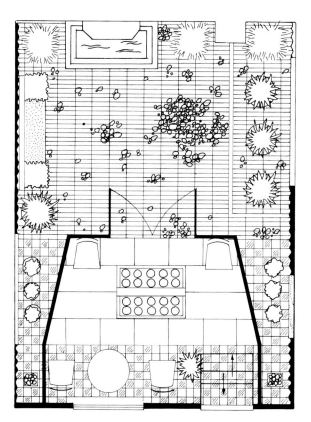

left *The plan shows how small the area set aside for the conservatory is, and how essential it was that the new structure should blend with the garden. Reflective materials, mirrors, and all-glass walls were used in the conservatory to make the limited space appear bigger.*

hydrangeas. White is the only colour allowed in this High Tech environment of glass and steel.

Not surprisingly, the walls of the garden are also partly made of metal. Galvanized corrugated sheeting, normally used as a roofing material, here provides a lightweight and durable vertical surface. Its shiny quality also contributes to the amount of light that reaches the garden. Indeed the single common denominator of all the materials used in the garden is that they are highly reflective and therefore project both reflected warmth and light into the garden and the conservatory.

These materials are also easy to work with, which is especially useful when access is restricted, as is the case with this garden. They are also much cleaner to use than more traditional building materials such as concrete paving blocks and bricks and mortar. In this project the standardization of the materials and their ease of construction made it possible for most of the garden to be fabricated off site and installed – rather like a fitted kitchen.

But it is the use of glass, in particular in the form of mirrors, that gives both the garden and the conservatory a deceptive sense of space. Two mirrors are fixed between two corrugated-steel panels, and when you look through the slightly reflective glass walls of the conservatory the illusion of an ever-repeating garden is produced. Mirror images pile up, creating a seemingly endless space.

right *In this view from inside the conservatory, the walls and roof of the almost all-glass structure are nearly invisible. A mirror, set between two panels of bright, galvanized corrugated iron, creates the illusion that the interior space extends well beyond its real confines. The white hydrangeas seem to be in the conservatory but are in fact outside.*

THE FULLER HOUSE

aNTOINE pREDOCK

When the designer is both an experienced architect and a landscape designer, it is not surprising that he regards architecture and landscape not separately but as a single entity. At this house in Phoenix, Arizona, not only are the indoor and outdoor spaces interrelated but both are also intimately connected with the world outside.

Antoine Predock describes his buildings and landscapes as "processional events, as choreographic events; they are an accumulation of vantage points both perceptual and experiential." As clients move from room to room, inside or outside a building, they are encouraged to experience different aspects of their surroundings. In the Fuller House, Predock has treated the house and its landscaping as a unified whole.

Looking across the valley in which Phoenix sits, the house is set against a range of rocky hills amid semi-desert scrubland. The surrounding landscape is flat and the only vegetation is cactus and scrub. The architectural forms belong to this landscape. The raw-stuccoed, uncoloured walls and elementary geometric forms characterize a style of building which draws upon the vernacular architecture of this part of Arizona and New Mexico. It is a style that is associated with traditional Mexican village architecture, pre-Columbian houses, and churches of the Spanish colonial era.

In order to connect the house and its landscaping to their environment, Predock based their layout on the movement of the sun, a significant force in the shaping of this region. The house has a morning wing and an evening wing, facing east and west respectively. These are united by an open-sided arcade which terminates at a pyramid and borders a large courtyard with a central round pool. Water runs into the pool through a channel after passing through boulders that climb up to and over the courtyard's plain-stuccoed perimeter wall. The channel follows a precise north–south axis. Near the pyramid a second narrow channel of water emerges from the house and flows into the pool

left *At the foot of the outside wall of the sunrise terrace a fountain creates a curtain of water. Facing due east, this side of the terrace provides a fine view of the rising sun. With its large, open windows and lattice-like roof, the terrace allows the residents to experience the beauty of both the sky and the expansive landscape.*

right *In this view down to the courtyard, water channels that are aligned along the north–south and east–west axes are clearly visible. Boulders direct a cascade of water into one channel and then into a circular pool. Piled up against and over the surrounding wall, they cleverly link the courtyard with the landscape beyond.*

at a right angle to the other channel, on an east–west axis. The two watercourses identify the alignment of the house within its environment. The whole complex is based on east–west and north–south axes, and the pool lies where these intersect.

The buildings wrap around three sides of the courtyard and on the fourth side a low wall extends from the pyramid to define the southern boundary. The wall is interrupted by a mass of randomly arranged stones and rocks, which are intended to form a link from the courtyard to the harsh terrain beyond. The pyramid, which is a study, is architecturally different from the rest of the building. The stepped pyramid has associations with ancient South American cultures but its glass top belongs firmly to the twentieth century.

In the courtyard no attempt has been made to create a planted area. Sand, rocks, and scrub continue the natural character of the external landscape and in some cases these are built around existing features. The boulders that form the waterfall spill into the pool, some resting on submerged steps, others completely under water. The cascade and the pool provide, alien to this environment, refreshing relief, rather like a waterhole.

The other exterior spaces, a sunrise terrace and a sunset tower, are open in form and echo the architecture of the house. Almost imperceptible as garden features, they are modern equivalents of the ornamental temple that was popular in the English landscape garden of the eighteenth and nineteenth centuries. The terrace is positioned at the end of the east wing. In front of the long, east-facing wall of the terrace there is a small fountain aligned in the direction of the rising sun. It consists of two stone-block pillars separated by a curtain of water that emerges from holes equally spaced on facing sides of the pillars.

On the west side, the tower is accessible only through the master bedroom and provides an uninterrupted view of the setting sun. Neither terrace nor tower has a roof, but each has a trellis-like steel canopy through which light passes and creates patterns on the stucco walls. Unglazed window-like openings in their walls provide views to east and west respectively. As well as providing a shaded and sheltered outdoor sitting area, the terrace and tower allow direct and close contact with the daily cycle of sunrise and sunset. This is a design that acknowledges both the sky and the surrounding landscape of mountains and desert.

right The house and its exterior space are designed around the rising and setting of the sun. Here the courtyard, with its circular pool and adjacent loggia, is illuminated at sunset. The pyramid-shaped study contributes to the sculptural quality of the space.

THEATRE OF THE TREES

aNTOINE pREDOCK

Antoine Predock is an architect and a landscape designer with a practice in Albuquerque, New Mexico. His work is often inspired by the landscape that surrounds his home, with its traditional style of building and its spectacular scenery. Of working in New Mexico he says: "Here one is aimed toward the sky and at the same time remains rooted in the earth with a geological and cultural past." This garden is an ideal example of Predock's design philosophy, even though it is to be found outside his familiar territory. *Theatre of the Trees* is situated in Dallas, Texas, and was created for clients who are keen birdwatchers.

On approaching the property one first encounters a rising block of huge limestone ledges, which Predock describes as "a weighty and earthbound foreground: a dam of expectation." The ledges are made of limestone found in the Austin Chalk Formation, which runs right through Dallas. These serve to remind the visitor of the relationship of the property to its location, in this case the edge of a steep wooded ravine. Stepped planting beds have been created in the tiers of limestone and are filled with plants to attract birds. The plants and birds of limestone areas like this are distinctive and specific, and even though no attempt has been made to use indigenous plant species, those selected are in character with the surrounding flora.

Almost every room of *Theatre of the Trees* has some form of access to the outside, to allow the occupants to take full advantage of the wonderful scenery and the wildlife. The roof is used as a viewing platform and has a circular skylight in it to allow light into the dining room below. It is even possible to enjoy a little birdwatching while eating a meal.

As is hinted at by the landscaping at the front, the house sits on the edge of a ravine, and there are spectacular views from this open side of the building. As well as designing the house with these vistas in mind, Predock gave it a "sky ramp." The most dramatic feature of the house, this is a logical extension of the ideas of the Renaissance architect and scholar Leone Battista

Alberti, whose ideas were to influence many of the gardens built in and around his native Florence at the time. In his treatise *De re aedificatoria*, completed in 1452, Alberti put forward the idea that house and garden should be treated as a whole and should both be part of the landscape. He drew heavily on the writings of the ancients, notably Vitruvius (active 46–30 BC), who believed that true beauty existed only as a harmony of all parts.

Sites for Renaissance villas and gardens were selected on the sides of hills so that they would have maximum exposure to the sun and wind and also afford extensive views. At the Villa Medici at Fiesole, near Florence, two terraces were constructed out of the hillside to command panoramic views of the landscape. Alberti himself designed the Villa Quaracchi, on the outskirts of Florence, for the merchant Giovanni Rucellai in 1459, incorporating all the principles outlined in his treatise. The surrounding moat and fish ponds were designed to be viewed from a raised, balustraded terrace. Elsewhere in the garden Alberti used the device of an extended pergola that reached beyond the garden by joining up

right The sky ramp launches out into the dense trees that grow in the ravine below. Made of black tensile steel, it is supported above a concrete "prow" that contains a manicured lawn. A circular room to the left has windows that wrap right around the structure, as well as a skylight, to give maximum light and visibility.

with an avenue of trees so that the patron could observe the river and the passing boats. The most advanced civil-engineering techniques of the day were employed in the construction in order to realize Alberti's ideas. Even so, in the Renaissance it would have been impossible to build anything like Predock's sky ramp.

Jutting out from a white concrete "prow" on the house, the structure penetrates a canopy of trees that grow on the sides of the ravine below. The ultimate in bird observatories, the sky ramp faces towards a nearby creek. This allows the owners to observe, from one place, birds in several different habitats without intruding or disturbing them. With its slender legs, the sky ramp resembles a pier, and it also functions like one, in this case providing promenade access over trees rather than water. This High Tech-inspired feature is made of black tensile-steel, and its floor is disconcertingly see-through, as it is made of perforated steel. According to Predock, the whole structure resonates with the wind. He describes the resulting sounds as almost like those of a musical instrument, and they blend perfectly with the sounds of the birds and the rustling of the trees all around.

The building does not attempt to sit unnoticed in its immediate environment. Indeed in its use of industrial materials and sharp, geometric concrete forms, it presents a direct contrast with the soft, lush landscape. However, Predock has exploited a property of the modern mirror-glass windows used on the curved rear wall in order to merge the house cleverly with its surroundings. When viewed from certain angles, the tall glass elevation reflects images of nearby trees, creating a High Tech camouflage effect that is produced by reflection rather than by the more usual paint.

The house has no garden in the usual sense and there are no areas designated for garden planting. There is, however, an area of cultivated lawn within the white-walled prow beneath the sky ramp and around the house a parkland-style landscape has been developed, with grass reaching right up to the walls.

Where it was necessary to excavate during the construction of the building, the disturbed ground was replanted with new trees, the species selected either matching or blending in with those already present in the ravine. Where possible, the trees that surround the house were retained, and some of these stand just outside the windows. Much of the original landscape of the site, with all its indigenous wildlife, was left untouched, and it was particularly important that the bird population should not be disturbed by the project.

In the absence of a conventional garden, the immediate environment of the house has been made into a garden simply by the presence of the architecture and structures, which provide access and views into it. Here the bird life is as important as plants are for the conventional gardener. This is a good example of a garden created by the co-option of nature.

THE GIBBS GARDEN

rOD bARNETT

In this garden in New Zealand the architecture of the house not only extends out to embrace the garden but also serves to define the garden's internal form. In this way the style of the house and of the garden are intimately linked. To achieve this, Rod Barnett has relied on the walled garden, an architectural element that has traditionally given protection and privacy but here also provides aesthetic unity.

The symbolic paradise gardens of ancient Persia were based on the idea of heaven brought to earth and were thought to need a surrounding wall to protect them from hostile earthly interference. Most Roman gardens were not contained by walls, the exception being the enclosed patio-style areas, completely surrounded by the house, found in the more affluent homes at Pompeii. Walled gardens reappeared in the Middle Ages as places in which to grow food and medicinal plants and then during the Renaissance they became a setting for luxurious displays of wealth.

England's landscape revolution in the eighteenth century banished the walled garden out of sight as solely a kitchen garden or cut-flower garden. Until then the garden wall had existed for a practical purpose, but by the twentieth century some designers were treating it as a design feature rather than merely using it to enclose the garden. In the 1940s the Mexican landscape architect Luis Barragán began to experiment with walls in this way. In his design for the Plaza del Bebedero de los Caballos, Las Arboledas, Mexico City (1958), he uses free-standing walls. A tall, rectangular white wall provides a backcloth for the shadows of trees, while a longer and lower, blue-painted wall beyond it suggests distance. For his scheme for the Plaza de las Fuentes, also in Mexico City, Barragán used walls to create a formal architectural framework that emphasizes the form and texture of the large boulders and exotic plants that are seen against them.

The white wall of the *Gibbs Garden* serves three purposes. It protects and provides privacy; it links the house to the garden visually; and, in its most contemporary role, it highlights the forms and textures of rocks and plants. Despite its modernity, this

garden is in the spirit of the Italian Renaissance garden ideal, whereby the house and garden were treated as a single visual entity. At that time the architectural style of the house was continued in the elements of the garden, and this produced order and symmetry in the garden's layout and proportions. Walls, terraces, and formal pools echoed the classical detailing of the house, and clipped hedges were shaped into geometric patterns.

In this twentieth-century garden the plain, white-rendered walls and the paved terrace continue the Modernist style of the house

left *Two attractively rounded boulders, echoes of the gravel garden, form stepping stones across the canal. Their natural form and texture conflict with the multicoloured tiles at the bottom of the watercourse to create additional interest.*

right *The view from the house reveals a garden divided into two distinct areas. A terrace is separated from a rock and gravel garden by a canal and a cascade of water. The architectural style of the house extends to the terrace and to the walls that confine and define the garden. The uniformity of the walls helps to bring order to a busy scene.*

into the garden. However, in the Gibbs Garden the Modernist values of simplicity and restraint are not continued throughout as they were in the Renaissance model. The walls and paving, in the plan, follow either a simple curved or angular line as they provide the garden with structure. But instead of the theme of restraint being continued in, for example, the use of a plain lawn, here an unexpected unrelated element is introduced – a large rock and gravel garden which pervades the whole garden. Even the plain surface of the terrace is not untouched, giving way to occasional pockets of planting and boulders. Also, unlike Italian gardens of the fifteenth and sixteenth centuries, which encouraged an extension of the garden into the natural landscape, here the garden is clearly sealed off from its surroundings. It contains a landscape very different from that visible beyond the wall.

The tall surrounding wall establishes privacy at garden level, and because of the property's elevated position it is also needed to provide shelter from the coastal winds. Long views are maintained by the stepping down of the wall that follows the natural slope of the land towards one corner and by the existence of an upper-storey balcony. In other places taller walls act as screens and backdrops for architectural planting and sculpture.

The clear lines and plain walls of the house, free of gratuitous decoration, indicate a Modernist style of domestic architecture, the white walls evoking the 1930s. The sets of concrete steps that lead down into the garden are almost Minimalist; handrails are either not used or are discreet. But the design of the garden is far from restrained, for it is full of movement and visual activity. The architectural language of the site, disciplined in the house, is given freedom in the garden, where it both defines and connects with other, very different landscape elements. It even provides platforms for an eclectic mix of sculpture and ornaments.

The garden is divided lengthways into two main areas. A curving terrace of pale and uniform paving wraps around the house and a lower rock and gravel garden, which extends to the perimeter wall. These two contrasting features are separated along almost their whole length by a canal and cascade of water. From the large French windows and nearby steps the eye is drawn along the curving line of the canal, which ends at a sculptural group of palms silhouetted by a high white wall behind them.

Following the curved, raised edge of the terrace, the water feature almost reaches the large doors that lead to the terrace. The canal is retained on the other side by a precise wall that belongs more in style to the house. A series of shallow steps also refers back to the house, in particular to the curved set of steps that are close by. The restrained Modernist appearance of the feature, however, is not maintained. In the water itself the unobtrusive black tiles that form the bottom of the canal suddenly give way to a random mix of dark-blue and pale-blue tiles, and, resting partially submerged, are occasional large, rounded stones, strays from the gravel garden.

The architectural simplicity of the overall design is deliberately interfered with by a number of random incidents. The terrace is equally cluttered. Pockets of planting, some large enough to accommodate palm trees, and more rocks are cut into the smooth floor at irregular intervals. A puzzling mix of planters and a strange collection of ornaments, including a skull, litter the floor.

This is a multi-cultural garden, where objects such as the skull and shell suggest a Maori influence, while other artefacts belong to the international world of modern sculpture. The gravel and rock garden hints at Japanese gardens, while the white, geometric walls belong to Western Modernist architecture.

The gravel and rock garden starts at a modern steel gate and runs the full length of the garden. It is sparsely planted with architectural exotics, including palms, cacti, agave, and several other succulents. Combined with the large boulders, in groups or isolated, these plantings create a complex environment of texture and sculptural form.

Throughout the garden the designer has introduced a number of still-life pictures. For example, the forms of a contemporary sculpture echo the leaf forms of a nearby palm tree. A large boulder straddles a rectangular carpet of succulent ground cover. On the terrace tall palm trees, a boulder, and a clump of ornamental grass create another vignette.

The function of the architecture as it extends out into the garden is to hold these details together and give the garden its structure. It provides an element of continuity, and makes the garden belong to the house both visually and literally. Although it is divisible into two main areas, terrace and rock garden, this is not a formal garden – a clearly defined and symmetrical arrangement. Instead, areas mingle. The rock garden is separated from the terrace by the canal but this does not prevent elements of it from reaching the house. Boulders traverse the walls, enter the canal, and come to rest on the terrace. The architecture moves outwards as the natural forms of the rock garden creep inwards.

Rod Barnett has created a garden which, although it displays the strong architectural forms that are an essential element of Modernism, is not impersonal. The submission of the Minimalist floors and walls to other influences has allowed room for the owners to add their own touches. This is a modern architectural garden that is fun to live with.

NAPA VALLEY RETREAT

bATTER kAY aSSOCIATES

The courtyard garden, a standard feature of the urban houses of ancient Rome, has been adapted for a "retreat" in Napa Valley, California. An indoor-outdoor garden was created inside, rather than outside, the four walls of the house, in order not to diminish the natural beauty of the immediate environment.

As you approach either of the long sides of the house you see what appear to be the doors of a garage. If you rolled them up you would find not a car but a hidden courtyard garden. The architects of this retreat have borrowed an idea first developed by the designers of houses in Roman times. Those ancient architects, needing to maximize the use of space in rapidly expanding cities and towns, put the garden within the house instead of around it.

There were two principal types of Roman garden: large, open gardens such as that created at Hadrian's villa at Tivoli, and enclosed gardens such as were found in urban environments such as Pompeii. In the first type the house was in the garden; in the second the architecture surrounded the garden like a room with no roof. Smaller Italian houses, such as those in Rome and at Pompeii, had been built around an atrium. An atrium was a

roofed and floored court with a central hole that allowed smoke to escape, below which there was an ornamental pond that collected the rainwater. Beyond the atrium there was always another enclosed space, this one completely open to the sky. It was called the *hortus* and was devoted to the production of vegetables. This now became a pleasure garden as an increasing proportion of Roman society enjoyed a lifestyle of wealth and leisure. The traditional design of the Roman house was thus modified to accommodate an internal garden.

The garden became an integral part of the framework of the house. A courtyard open to the sky was surrounded on all four sides by a covered walkway, or portico, complete with a colonnade. The columns of the portico were often connected by a low wall. In the centre, recalling the earlier atrium, there was

right A view of the courtyard garden looking towards the main living quarters. The galvanized corrugated-steel walls glimmer with the reflected light and colours of the surrounding trees and sky. To the left a glimpse through a garage-style door reveals the wilder, untouched landscape that lies outside the house.

below The ground plan reveals the unusual tapered shape of the building. The courtyard garden is immediately to the right of the rectangle forming the visitors' quarters, in the broken line.

usually a fountain, from which paths would radiate in a symmetrical pattern. The substantial remainder of the garden was given over to lush planting. Rooms such as the library or dining hall would face the garden, their exterior walls often painted with murals depicting views of distant landscapes in order to create a greater sense of space. The Roman courtyard garden gave the house light and air and provided ease of movement between rooms. Surrounded by the house, the garden was also private and secure. Considering these virtues, and particularly the economical use of space, it is surprising that the Roman idea is not more prevalent in domestic architecture today.

Unlike the Roman peristyle garden, where there were rooms on all four sides of the courtyard, the accommodation at this retreat is only on two sides. On one side there is a pair of large, garage-style doors and on the other a single one, which, when rolled up, frames the rugged natural landscape of exposed boulders and trees that surrounds the house. The imaginary landscapes that were painted on the walls of Roman courtyards are not needed here. When the doors are shut the courtyard garden is totally enclosed and secure. When they are open it provides a link between the indoor and the outdoor, between domestication and the uncultivated wilderness beyond. In fact the coarse grass, weeds, and indigenous plants of the exterior landscape have been allowed to re-establish themselves right up to the building. The creation of the garden within the confines of the house allowed the external natural environment to be left almost as found. After all, the whole point of a retreat is to be at one with nature rather than to impose a design upon it.

The roofless courtyard garden lies between the main house and the guest quarters, and the doors of adjoining rooms open onto the space, allowing easy access to various rooms. It is paved, but pockets of earth have been left for planting, including small-growing trees. As in the Roman model, there is even a fountain in the centre. The garden's walls are clad in galvanized corrugated steel. This material's shiny surface increases the light in the garden, reflects the surrounding tall trees, and responds to the sky's changing colours. Large, rectangular, floor-to-ceiling windows open onto the garden and provide its other "walls." The garden is a meeting place, just as the Roman version was, as well as an outside room complete with dining table and chairs

Many contemporary garden designers, notably John Brookes, have developed the idea of the garden room, interpreting it to mean the garden as an extension of the house. Here this concept is reversed. The simple omission of a roof makes the enclosed architectural space into a garden.

A PHOTOGRAPHER'S RETREAT

nIALL mcLAUGHLIN

The usual buildings found at the bottom of a garden, such as a shed, greenhouse, or child's "den," are unlikely to have any pretensions as architecture. But in this garden in Northamptonshire, England, the architect Niall McLaughlin has extended the idea of the home-built shed to create a waterside studio for a photographer.

Aquatic insect life was the subject of much of the photographer's work, so it seemed a good idea to site the "shack," as the architect calls it, near water. There was a pond at the far end of the garden, but it was stagnant and had been abandoned to weed and brambles. This was cleared and brought back to life with the help of oxygenating, marginal, and bog plants, and fish.

The studio was constructed over the edge of the pond and extends out to one side. In addition to providing a hide for wildlife photography, it is also a peaceful place to which the whole family can escape. Equipped with sleeping quarters and a sauna, it is like a second home at the bottom of the garden.

Sitting inside, among the marginal planting, one enjoys a close-up view of both pond and garden. Unlike a conservatory, which by definition is built onto a house, the studio is detached from the photographer's home and is connected to the landscape instead. One sees the garden from within rather than from afar. In this respect the shack has much in common with the teahouses and pavilions built in large gardens in northern Europe during the nineteenth century. These provided shelter and comfort so that the garden could be enjoyed from a position away from the house whatever the weather. Architecturally, they were often eccentric and eclectic, with little resemblance to the house.

This building is similarly unconventional. No detailed construction drawings were made: there was simply a model and a collage of visual ideas. The construction evolved rather as an imaginative child would build a den or treehouse by improvising with the materials to hand; for example, corrugated oil drums filled with concrete were used to make stepping stones across the pond. This slightly ramshackle approach helps the studio to sit easily in its

above *A glimpse through the window provides a close view of the pond and the marginal planting of ligularias and variegated grasses. In the centre is an improvised stepping stone. To the right is a deck for mooring a boat.*

right *To the left is the main entrance, reached by an informal path that weaves its way through polygonums, ligularias, and rushes. In the centre perforated metal canopies cover skylights. At the far right is the sauna.*

rural setting, as does the inspiration for this unusual construction. During the Second World War the local farmland was used as a base for US air reconnaissance. Black B-24 bombers flew from here on secret missions and one of these, dismantled, is buried close to the pond. The studio's plan drawing hints strongly at a broken aircraft, with crumpled wings and fuselage, that has come to rest beside a pool. From a distance, in elevation, the building does look like a fantastic flying machine. The cockpit-like structure on the roof acts like a glass lantern to spread soft light, suitable for photography, into the studio below.

The segmented, wing-like roof can move in the wind, a useful feature as strong winds are common in this part of the world, and this responsiveness to the elements further connects the studio to its environment. A highly experimental combination of fibreglass, polycarbonate, plywood, and metal was used for the roof, which is fixed to the ground by steel rods that bend the flat sheets into a graceful curve.

Whether the building looks like an old war plane or even some strange insect hovering over the pond is open to debate. What is certain is that it is visually striking and appropriate to its site. It shows that, with imagination, even a humble piece of architecture can contribute both aesthetically and practically to a garden.

above A triangular, semi-opaque "wing" gives shade to the southern corner of the building. The "cockpit" admits diffused light into the building. The mooring deck and the sauna are visible on the left.

below A schematic plan shows the studio's location at the top-left side of the pond. This drawing is one of only a handful made for the job. Construction of the building was mainly improvised from a model and images from source material.

right Looking like a fantastic flying machine complete with wings and cockpit, the studio sits at the bottom of a garden that looks onto farmland. Its ramshackle appearance helps it to blend into its agricultural surroundings. From a distance it appears to have landed gently and nestled into a green hollow.

INSTANT GRATIFICATION

INSTANT GRATIFICATION

New technology brings constant changes to our lives and the pace of change quickens all the time. Speed, whether in food, communications, or long-distance travel, is seen as indispensable in today's developed world. Accompanying the idea of "instant" consumer products and services is that of "throwaway" goods. In the 1960s paper was developed which could be used to make disposable clothes, and "designer" paper jackets, a series produced by the Tate Gallery in London that are now collectable items. Designers in a wide range of fields contributed to the dominance of the transitory over the long-lasting and to the acceptance of built-in obsolescence. Perhaps the perfect example of the new attitude towards design was the inflatable chair, also from the 1960s. To use it you pumped it up, and when it was no longer needed you deflated it and packed it away.

While the concepts of instantaneity, disposability, and constant change are now associated with most areas of contemporary design, they had until recently no relevance to the garden. The predominant notion of the garden was of a place in which to grow plants, shrubs, and trees, and this process had determined the length of time a garden took to create. This, combined with a tendency, in Europe at least, to look to history for inspiration, meant that speed was not sought after. This outlook has long encouraged the use of natural materials, such as wood and stone, that will weather well as the garden matures. Even the designers of Modernist gardens of the 1930s and 1950s in the USA used methods of construction and planting practices intended to achieve long-term rather than immediate solutions.

This approach was appropriate in the eighteenth century, when "Capability" Brown was creating great landscaped gardens in England. His clients were the new, wealthy property owners who were establishing their family seats. They were happy to invest in gardens that would be fully appreciated only by the following generations. Only then would the hundreds of trees Brown deployed have reached maturity and created the desired effect.

For today's homeowner life is very different. The private house is smaller and so is the garden, but more significant is the fact that few family homes are passed on to the next generation. More

often our stay is short as a result of work commitments or simply a desire for change. Movement is becoming international as it grows easier to set up home in a different country. Many people, particularly when living abroad, prefer the flexibility offered by rented accommodation. But if they wish to create and enjoy gardens, the conventional long-term garden is clearly unsuitable. This more mobile lifestyle is a good reason for making a more instant garden, but is justification needed for creating a garden that looks at its best from the day it is finished?

Instead of cumbersome, time-consuming, labour-intensive materials and methods, why not use lightweight, prefabricated, and quickly assembled alternatives? By combining these with container-grown specimen plants you can create a garden in hours rather than days. If your stay is to be short, why not make the garden portable so that you can take it with you, along with your other possessions, when you move? Fortunately, there are contemporary garden designers who are responding to this challenge and can provide inspiration.

The new thinking has, to an extent, been stimulated by the work of a number of contemporary fine artists who, from as early as the 1960s, have been extending the boundaries of sculpture to create temporary works of art in the natural environment. These outdoor art installations demonstrate how the character of the landscape can be transformed by additions that are often quick and simple. In Rococo Wood the American artist Mara Adamitz Scrupe has redefined a small, overgrown, neglected corner of a

left The Moving Garden *(1999), designed by Peter Kukorelli, a student at the Royal College of Art, London, is intended as a way of improving the experience of travelling on public transport. The witty design is a fusion of tram and garden, and it includes plants on the roof and grass on the stairs. Perhaps the ordinary caravan or camper van could be converted to accommodate a similar portable garden.*

left *The creators of this exhibit at the Festival International des Jardins at Chaumont-sur-Loire instantly expanded the apparent size of the garden by the clever use of mirrors. Not only do these reflect and extend the planting of cornflowers and clipped dwarf hedging in which they sit, but they also reflect and introduce into the garden the landscape that lies beyond.*

right *Chandeliers sealed within acrylic cases and suspended from trees constitute an artwork by Mara Adamitz Scrupe. They are illuminated for three hours during the early evening by a solar-power system devised by the artist. Intended to "bring the inside outside," they are an example of how artists are contributing to the concept of the garden. Here the designer has produced an installation that is temporary but effective.*

wooded landscape by introducing suspended solar-powered chandeliers, each within a weather-tight clear acrylic case. The elegant and decorative lanterns, which in style belong to a bygone era, instantly create a sense of a place that is full of mystery, where flickering lights evoke the ghosts of the past.

The American Martha Schwartz, who trained as both an artist and a landscape architect, has been quicker than most to respond to developments in the fine arts. Her approach, which in many cases is closer to environmental art than landscape design, has brought her invitations to create a number of instant and

temporary "installations." At the World Financial Center in New York, as part of an event called the New Urban Landscape, she made the instant and temporary Turf Parterre garden. The design of the parterre mimicked the arrangement of the square windows of the building. Squares of turf were cut from the existing lawn at the foot of the building to mirror the pattern of the windows. The parterre did not stop there, but continued up the façade of the tall structure, with squares of Astroturf replacing the real thing. This willingness to cross between disciplines is a characteristic of New Tech garden designers. In the case of Schwartz it has led to

her being commissioned to design a novel kind of landscape garden that has hosted a wide range of events from World Cup football to a family wedding.

For many garden designers the opportunity to develop the "instant" garden is provided by flower shows and "show gardens," both of which are by nature instant and transient. At the Chelsea Flower Show in London the guiding principle is horticultural wizardry, and seemingly established gardens are created in weeks. At the Festival International des Jardins at Chaumont-sur-Loire in France and at London's Hampton Court

Flower Show greater emphasis is placed on innovation and experimentation. But the creators of such gardens are not the first instant gardeners. Historical precedent was set in the late seventeenth century by Louis XIV of France in his magnificent garden of Le Grand Trianon at Versailles. In a defining moment in the history of gardening, he defied the restrictions imposed by the seasons. Flowers were taken from the greenhouse and bedded out temporarily on some of the coldest days of the year. This was often done at lunchtime, allowing the king to show his guests around a summer garden during an afternoon in the middle of winter.

THE NOMADIC VEGETABLE GARDEN

pATRICK nADEAU, vINCENT dUPONT-rOUGIER & jOELLE aLEXANDRE

This portable and easily installed garden could provide a solution for those for whom
a permanent garden is impossible or imprudent. A fusion of science and art, it was
created by a team including an architect and an industrial development consultant
for the 1999 Festival International des Jardins, held at Chaumont-sur-Loire, France.

*below White aubergines
flourish on the elevated deck
of the Nomadic Vegetable
Garden. They are planted not
in soil but in mineral wool, an
inert, fibrous growing medium,
and are fed and watered by a
soilless hydroponic system.*

In today's mobile society many people rent their homes and,
even if they have the time, have little inclination to invest in any
permanent feature, such as a traditional, long-term garden, at a
temporary address. Moreover, rented accommodation, whether
it is a ground-floor flat with a concrete backyard or even a
penthouse with only a roof terrace, is often not suitable for any
garden other than an instant one using containers for growing.
There is a clear need for a purpose-built portable garden.

Decorative shrubs and herbaceous plants can improve the look
of a backyard, roof terrace, or small garden, but it also possible
to make a portable, container-based vegetable garden in places
where space is limited. By providing food, this sort of garden can
save money. It is easy to maintain and satisfying, and has the
further benefit that many vegetables are decorative. Herbs can
be included, and as well as giving fresh flavour to food, these
can be fragrant and attractive.

The Nomadic Vegetable Garden takes the idea of container
growing into the realm of horticultural science. Concentrating on
food crops, this experimental portable garden explores the use
of above-the-ground cultivation techniques. Plant supports,
atomizers, water circuits, and screens for protection against bad
weather have all been specifically designed for this garden, which
has a built-in irrigation system. Water is recovered and enriched
with nutritional elements, if needed, in a tarpaulin suspended
under the central floor. It is then drawn up and pumped back
into the feed circuit.

When not in use the garden looks like a large, stainless-steel
cube perched on a simple undercarriage. The four sides of the
cube open to reveal four wooden decks, which are the different
areas of the garden. A deck on one side can be pulled down
from the vertical, closed position to the horizontal to form an
articulated greenhouse made from clear plastic sheeting. A second
deck has an extendable trellis, and a third contains rows of
mineral wool, an artificial growing medium, under a partial

*right With its sides fully extended, the garden provides three
decks, each purpose-built to encourage growth above the ground
of a wide variety of fruit, vegetables, and herbs. In the foreground
lettuces do well between weed-suppressing porcelain tiles. To the
left a lightweight, fold-away greenhouse provides a perfect
environment for tomato plants.*

canopy. On these three decks vegetables, fruit, and herbs have been planted and are growing courtesy of a system of hydroponics. This is a soilless method of cultivation in which the plants are placed in mineral wool, through which water containing dissolved inorganic nutrient salts is pumped. Salads and basil grow in shallow troughs of mineral wool covered with porcelain tiles to prevent weed growth. Aubergines ripen under the plastic roof and tomatoes in the open air on the trellised platform. The fourth deck is a terrace for rest and leisure and for enjoying the fruits of one's labour.

Although this garden is not truly instant, as the vegetables have to be planted and allowed to grow in their own time, it takes only a few hours to set up the three planting decks. At the end of the season the whole garden can be folded back into a cube and towed away. Because it incorporates new technology that does not require soil, it can be erected in any place where there is adequate space. There are also further benefits. As the planting is up in the air it is free from ground pests such as slugs and snails and there are no problems with soil-borne disease-causing pathogens. The table-height planting surfaces are useful for those who find bending down difficult.

This garden is part of a wider research programme into soil-free plant culture that is being carried out by its designers. Its technology could shape the urban garden of the future and bring sustainable relief to drought-stricken Third World countries.

above This coloured sketch plan shows the simple but efficient design of this movable garden. From a central cube four decks are pulled down. Three of them form a vegetable garden, while the fourth is a place in which to relax, complete with a deckchair and a canopy to provide shelter and shade.

right At night the garden looks rather like a lunar landing craft. Fully opened, the decks of the garden and sitting area are suspended above the ground by retractable cables and bars fixed to four central columns. Extendable blinds provide shade during the day.

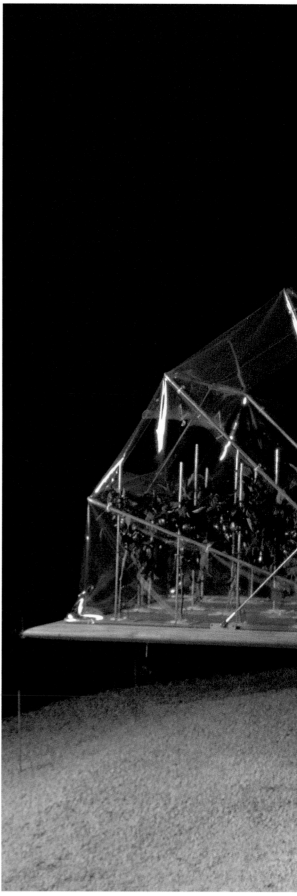

GROWING VISION

bONITA bULAITIS, jULIA fOGG & SUSAN SANTER

With its unusual materials and equally unorthodox method of construction, this inventive garden could provide the ideal answer for young people who would like to add outdoor living spaces to their homes but lack the time or money to set about making traditional, permanent gardens.

The *Growing Vision* garden, designed and built by a talented young team, was created at London's Hampton Court Flower Show in 1995. At that time it was regarded as shocking by visitors to the show, most of the horticulturally inclined seeing it as a challenge to the traditional purpose and nature of a garden.

This was mainly because the garden was not predominantly about plants and had few defined planting areas. In addition it was made from materials that are more often seen on a building site than in a garden. A related objection concerned the method of construction. The apparently casual way in which the project was put together implied a lack of craftsmanship and permanence that most traditionalists felt contradicted the ethos of the garden. Although all gardens at flower shows and garden festivals are short-term affairs, they are designed to give the opposite impression. Mature plants, solid walls, and heavy stone paving, often distressed to make it look old and weathered, all combine to suggest gardens that have been there forever and will remain so. Ambitious rockeries and waterfalls, presented as if they were part of an unspoiled landscape, are another element in this sleight of hand. Many show gardens take weeks to build, only to be destroyed at the end of the event. They are not made from materials that allow them to be reconstructed elsewhere. One of the principal advantages of *Growing Vision* is that it could easily be removed and reused.

The most distinctive feature of this garden is also the most challenging. Occupying the central space is a framework constructed from steel scaffolding tubes. These are not fixed together permanently but are simply held by scaffolding clips. The structure uses only standard-length scaffolding tubes. None of these was cut to length to suit the design of the framework as this would have incurred the wrath of the scaffolding suppliers.

The main purpose of this tubular structure is to provide a novel elevated area for sitting, or rather perhaps sunbathing. High up, the user is out of sight of people in nearby gardens as well as above the unwanted shade cast by surrounding trees. The structure is very basic and its contents are slightly reminiscent of the style of interior design used in the Habitat stores by their creator, Terence Conran, in the UK in the early 1970s. The hallmarks of these were functional design and a preference for the plain rather than the patterned.

Access to the upper area of the structure is gained via an ordinary ladder, just as on a building site. The floor consists simply of eight timber planks resting on the steel frame, and scaffolding also provides a rudimentary handrail. What makes this simple platform attractive is the colourful scatter cushions and bean bags, inviting to collapse into on a sunny day. The modern synthetic fabric used to make the cushions is weatherproof and resistant to water and they and the bean bags could be left outside without fear of their deteriorating. Hanging from the structure and fixed to the floor are fabric drapes. These add a sense of volume to its very linear form and can be swivelled round to provide temporary privacy or shade. Like the cushions, they bring colour and a sense of theatre to the garden.

Of a more permanent nature is the glass screen at the rear of the garden. This is made from structural glass bricks bonded together. The development of the glass brick led to its frequent use in twentieth-century modernist architecture. Its modular form and graph paper-like appearance when used in quantity, along

below *A scaffolding frame and a simple deck of wooden planks reached by a ladder make an unusual sunbathing platform. Furnished with colourful cushions and bean bags, it is a space that is likely to appeal more to the young than to the older generation.*

with its ability to form both curved and straight walls, appealed to architects who sought a geometric and less decorative style. It has also become a useful ingredient in High Tech design.

The glass bricks create a self-supporting wall through which light can pass but which is almost impossible to see through and therefore provides privacy. Within the context of a garden a translucent glass wall has a further advantage – because it does not block out light, it prevents the shading of borders that are planted against north-facing walls. The reflective surface also provides visual interest as its appearance changes all the time as the sun moves across the sky.

On the ground identical glass bricks are used in a solely decorative fashion, in combination with small concrete tiles and gravel. These all form hard surfaces which, along with ground-cover planting in the pockets of gravel, replace the familiar lawn altogether. Many of the ground-cover plants are tough enough to withstand being walked over occasionally. This makes the whole garden available for leisure use. For anyone who is interested in this garden as an inexpensive option, the fact that no lawnmower is needed could also be an important consideration.

The informal and improvised appearance of the garden, with its casual furnishings, conjures up students' living quarters. Even the planters littered around the garden are simply recycled rustproof tin cans. The designers have taken ideas associated with setting up one's first home away from home and adapted them to the garden. Here the principal design decisions were dictated by the aim to achieve both portability and fast results. As much of the planting is in portable raised planters, the garden could quickly and easily be reconstructed for use in rented accommodation with a small backyard or plot.

Handmade timber pergolas and arbours, along with specially cut and carved stone used to form the edges of terraces and ornamental pools, characterized the great historic gardens. Even the respected modern gardens of the twentieth century called for a considerable investment of time and expenditure on good-quality materials. However, many people living in temporary accommodation lack the time, money, or indeed space to invest in a permanent garden constructed to exacting specifications. Much more suitable and appropriate to their lifestyle is the low-budget, self-built, and temporary solution provided here by three imaginative designers. But although it was designed primarily for the younger generation, this is perhaps a project for people of any age who want an unusual garden in which they can relax and have fun.

below For the ground surface of the garden the designers created an area that displays a variety of textures. Concrete tiles are combined with an imaginative use of glass blocks. The hard surface is softened by ground-cover planting in the gravelled areas.

right Blue sails hang from the scaffolding structure, giving substance to its sparse linear form. They also serve to provide shade and privacy for the "ground floor" of the garden. To the rear a wall made of glass bricks is an effective screen, forming a barrier without creating shade.

THE LITTMAN WEDDING GARDEN

mARTHA sCHWARTZ

One of America's most influential and controversial contemporary landscape architects transformed a garden so that two keen gardeners could celebrate their wedding there. This striking example of the instant but temporary garden is both appropriate for the occasion and an enchanting piece of landscaping.

Martha Schwartz studied fine arts and landscape architecture at the University of Michigan and Harvard Graduate School of Design. This broad creative education helps her to approach her present discipline with an open mind. Her many commissions combine an inventive use of new and unlikely materials with visual ideas that are often wry and witty. A grand wedding provided an opportunity for the experimentation she enjoys.

The Littmans' family home at Deal on the New Jersey coast was to stage the wedding of their son. Schwartz was already redesigning the garden and her immediate aim was to make the partly dismantled garden look presentable for the big occasion. Its transitional state allowed her team great freedom in creating a temporary garden. They could even paint the grass and areas of concrete as these were about to be ripped up.

Since the bride and the groom both loved gardening, this became the theme of their "wedding garden." Astroturf, flowerpots, and potted plants were some of the basic ingredients used to develop the gardening theme. But it was the extensive use of paint as an instant floor covering that was the most significant device in transforming this large garden.

The layout was based on the sequence of events scheduled for the wedding day. Spaces were designed to complement specific events, from the procession, through the wedding ceremony, which was also to be held outdoors, to the reception and the

below The plan shows how the garden was divided to accommodate the events of the wedding. At the bottom a long walkway leads to the tent where the ceremony took place. At the top left is the swimming pool, converted into a reception area; at the top right is the banqueting tent, with the Sunflower Grove just below it.

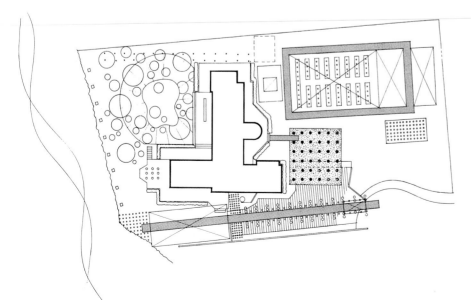

right The Sunflower Grove was created as a place where guests could stroll and mingle after arriving for the wedding or during pauses in the proceedings. An area of concrete, gravel, and grass was unceremoniously coated in paint to form a clearly defined rectangular space. Orderly lines of sunflowers bundled in pots create criss-cross avenues and wittily convey the gardening theme.

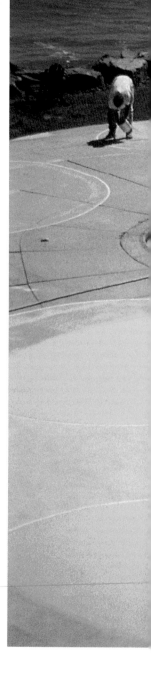

banquet. On arriving guests were invited to mingle and stroll in the Sunflower Grove. Here the gravel, concrete, and grass of the existing garden were unified by the application of purple-pink paint covering a 12m (40ft) square. Within this area were placed, in neat rows, thirty-six 1.5m (5ft) tall bundles of sunflowers held upright in pots. It is easy to imagine the White Rabbit from *Alice in Wonderland* turning up at any time.

The adjacent Long Walkway marked the beginning of the ceremony. The wedding procession made its way down a 45m (150ft) long carpet of Astroturf, lined on both sides by sixty 2.4m (8ft) tall conifers. The path finally passed through ordered lines of empty flowerpots painted blue on the inside to mirror the ocean beyond. The ceremony took place in a simple white tent with a view of the sea as a backdrop. To provide an area for the reception the concrete surround of the swimming pool was enlivened with an abstract pattern of bright-yellow circles, many of which spread out over the adjoining lawn and patio. Even in the banqueting tent the gardening theme was continued, with

tables covered in white linen playing host to a neat row of orange trees, their foliage clipped into balls. Each tree was potted in a clear acrylic cylinder so that its roots were visible.

This garden was fanciful and frivolous, designed to foster a party atmosphere, but the idea of transforming a space instantly and temporarily can also be of use elsewhere. A dull, uninviting concrete backyard of a rented house or flat can be rapidly transformed with brightly coloured paint, potted plants (real or even fake), and Astroturf or other synthetic floor coverings (such

as recycled rubber matting). This is especially useful if one's stay is to be brief. Water-based paints will cover most surfaces, but for a more temporary finish it is best to use wash-off theatre floor paint.

Traditionally, a garden is a long-term project intended to solve the problems of the site and meet the needs of its users. But in the *Littman Wedding Garden* Martha Schwartz proves that it can be both temporary and effective. In this inventive assemblage of found objects, paint, and potted plants she has transformed ordinary spaces by the imaginative use of commonplace materials.

THE SOFT GARDEN

THE SOFT GARDEN

Not all contemporary architecture and three-dimensional design is concerned with the use of hard-edged or high-precision materials. Developments in the chemical industry have led to the creation of thermoplastics, which can be moulded into all kinds of organic shapes. New synthetic fibres, many of them by-products of the space race, have encouraged an adventurous application of "soft" materials in art, architecture, and design. Inflatable buildings and tent-like roofing are commonplace. Many of the new fabrics have already played a discreet role in the landscaping and horticultural industry. The so-called "geo-textiles" have been used in ground stabilization and the control of weeds. Other new fabrics have been used to make windbreaks that have proved more successful and more economical than traditional fences or walls.

The term "soft furnishings" usually refers to rugs, carpets, and curtains, but in the 1960s some furniture became "soft." In the years following the Second World War the austere wartime utility specifications for furniture had gradually been abandoned and the increasing affluence of the 1950s provided an opportunity for indulgence in design. Chairs, in particular, took on a more relaxed look, in which any rigid sub-structure was lost beneath extensive

below This garden, entitled Just What Is It, was made for the 1991 Hampton Court Flower Show. Among its many unusual features are soft fittings. Seating is provided by a weather-proof bean bag and there is a soft planter made from a plastic-coated fabric.

right *In this sculpture, entitled* Colourscape, *architecture and art combine to create a womb-like organic environment. Nearly one hundred highly coloured chambers are linked by elliptical openings to form a labyrinth of colour and space illuminated by daylight. Soft, sensual, walk-through sculptures of this kind have inspired a few adventurous modern garden designers.*

upholstered padded forms and fat cushions. Towards the end of the 1950s even office furniture lost its rigidity and became more organic and curvilinear in form. The most famous office chair of all must be the Egg chair, designed in 1959 by Arne Jacobsen. This swivel chair is remembered as a frequent prop in many films, including the James Bond series and the late-sixties science-fiction classic *2001: A Space Odyssey*. Its womb-like character and organic shape were achieved through the way it was made. It consisted of a fabric-covered, foam-upholstered, moulded-fibreglass shell on an aluminium swivel base with a loose seat cushion. A version in plain, bright-red fabric was the most popular.

The emergence in the 1960s of a youth culture, particularly among a growing student population with limited living space, also contributed to the evolution of styles of furniture that were less formal and less expensive. Few student flats in the 1960s and 1970s lacked a bean bag, a large floor cushion made from a fabric bag filled with polystyrene beads.

Painters have always been concerned with depicting softness and in the twentieth century Dadaist and Surrealist artists pursued their own interpretations of this quality. Salvador Dali's 1931 painting *The Persistence of Memory*, with its melting watches, has proved to be a particularly enduring image. This illusionistic transformation of a hard object into a soft one was developed more literally in a sculpture by the German-Swiss artist Meret Oppenheim, whose *Lunch in Fur* (1936) consisted of a tea cup, spoon, and saucer covered in fur fabric. The idea of wrapping was developed on a large scale from the 1950s by the artist Christo and his partner Jeanne-Claude, who used rope and modern polyester fabric to package whole buildings (including the Reichstag in Berlin), trees, paths and even a rocky part of Australia's coastline.

Garden designers have always worked with soft materials. In the context of the garden, the term "soft landscaping" formerly referred to the modelling of the natural landscape, and the creation of lawns and planted areas, although not all shrubs and trees can be described as soft. Now, however, it is also applied to the hard landscape – paving, walls, furniture, and even buildings – for new robust, weather-proof "soft" materials are contributing to the look of the garden. In the form of outdoor scatter cushions, soft planters, and fabric screens and canopies, they add a note of playfulness and informality. Plastic or rubber matting can even provide a soft alternative to concrete paving.

A soft garden need not imply the use of soft furnishings and building materials. Inspired by the languid and liquid forms of the Surrealist artists Jean Arp and Joan Miró, the Brazilian designer Roberto Burle Marx created some of the twentieth century's most modern gardens. Hard surfaces are given organic forms and combined with irregularly shaped pools of single-colour planting. The effect is one of a sumptuous abstract painting. Hard landscape features can also be made to look soft. Martha Schwartz, in a homage to the Uniroyal Tire and Rubber Company, the former occupants of a site that she was working on, installed tyre-shaped concrete rings as seats around hundreds of date palms.

Today New Tech garden designers are exploring the potential of softness in the garden. The California-based designer Mia Lehrer extends the possibilities of conventional soft landscaping while the Vietnamese-American artist Andy Cao proves that even fragments of glass can be used to make a soft garden.

above Tyre-like rings at the bases of rows of date palms provide unusual seating in this scheme in Commerce, California, devised by the landscape architect and artist Martha Schwartz. The tyres are not as soft as they might seem – they are made of concrete, painted white.

right Billowing woven polyester fabric restrained by ropes transforms the appearance of the trees about which it is wrapped in this artwork created by Christo and Jeanne-Claude for the Fondation Beyeler in Switzerland. Temporary packaging did not harm the trees but exaggerated their form by concealing their inner structure. Soft landscaping has been rendered even softer.

VOYAGE OF VITALITY

bONITA bULAITIS

A garden designer who comes from a different background from most has created a landscape that is both sensitive and evocative. By combining theatrical elements, such as dramatic lighting, with intriguing structural features in metal and stone, she has produced a garden that invites visitors to explore its every nook and cranny.

Bonita Bulaitis is one of very few contemporary garden designers whose background is not in horticulture or landscape design. She trained and practised as a graphic designer and consequently her work is not constrained by the practical baggage of gardening. Her introduction to garden design came through an interest in growing container plants and her planting skills developed during a period spent creating hanging baskets and containers for a garden centre. This was followed by a course at a garden design school, after which she set up her own business.

To the rear of the *Voyage of Vitality* garden an elevated, stage-like area is reached by a series of steps whose risers conceal rows of lights. This is both an attractive and a practical device in a garden that is intended to be used in the evenings. On the elevated platform sits a sinuous wooden bench on almost wire-thin metal legs. To the rear of the bench is a series of wedge-shaped panels, arranged in a fan-like fashion to form a screen of blue and copper. The copper edging and veining in the panels are a theme continued in the series of stark spikes of copper pipe that form an open boundary amid the planting to the rear. The garden contains many elements that have a theatrical appearance and this aspect of the design is reinforced by the use of dramatic lighting to illuminate the space at night. But what most lends this garden its distinctive character is the subtle treatment of the ground. Here the angular forms of the rear screen give way to a sensuous and original treatment of both the hard and the soft landscaping.

Tones of copper and bronze are a recurring colour theme in this and other gardens that Bulaitis has created. These colours appear in both planting and artefacts and occur again in this garden in the soft landscaping around the lower pool area.

right Knitted wire and sequin ribbons spiral unevenly around thin steel rods. The spring coils are weighted at the bottom with silver pear drops, which causes them to bounce when agitated by the wind. The features sit in the water and tone in with the surrounding planting. Subtle coppers and bronzes are a repeated colour theme in the garden.

above Sunray-shaped tentacles reaching out into the stream suggest sandbanks, but are made of quartzite stone bonded with solid resin. This technique produces features which, although natural and soft in appearance, are hard-wearing and permanent. Coloured particles can be introduced into the mixture – in this case blue in the watercourse – to heighten the colour's impact.

left At the rear of the watercourse two solid blue spheres pick up the colour of the pigment that is embedded in and around this feature. The planting here consists of hardy grasses such as Stipa tenuissima, *massed together with low-maintenance perennials such as achillea and penstemon. The evergreen sage* Salvia officinalis purpurea *softens the edges of the watercourse.*

The dense surrounding planting of grasses and perennials is complemented by fine steel rods with ingenious and delicate knitted-wire and sequinned-ribbon spirals coiling around them. The spirals expand and contract in diameter as they hang down. Small, silver pear drops are suspended from the ends and on windy days the springiness of the spirals makes these bob up and down.

The hard surface at the centre of the garden looks from a distance like fine gravel, but it is in fact resin bonded with quartzite stone. This creates a solid, hard-wearing surface that is also natural and organic-looking and has the advantage that it can be moulded into almost any form. In this case it is cast into tentacles suggesting sunrays, which poke out from the main hard areas and paths into the watercourse. The process of resin bonding also allows coloured particles to be incorporated into the surfaces; here blue granules line the bottom of the watercourse and its margins. Creating this series of structured, soft sandbanks would have been impossible using just gravel, while concrete would not have given the natural-looking, soft surface texture.

In her gardens Bulaitis uses a repertoire of shrubs and perennials that are both hardy and easy to look after. Even her show gardens, if made permanent, would be tough and easily maintained, at the same time as looking stylish and colourful.

The use of sweeps of mixed hardy grasses and perennials to create low-maintenance garden and parkland schemes is a late-twentieth-century innovation. It was pioneered by Wolfgang Oehme and James van Sweden, who first employed it in their home city of Washington DC in the late 1990s. Van Sweden's

background in architecture and planning is the driving force behind the sweeping shapes and precise execution of their projects, while Oehme's training as a nurseryman and his interest in gardening as an extension of ecology are influential in the planting choices the pair make. Their distinctive style uses a limited repertoire of plants and their philosophy is that plants must earn their place in any scheme. In the USA there is no culture of painstaking garden maintenance of the kind that has long existed in Europe and particularly in Britain, and the clients of designers such as van Sweden and Oehme do not expect to have to constantly tend their plants. To earn their places plants must be hardy, disease-resistant, drought-tolerant, showy, need little extra support and ideally look good for most of the year. Hardy grasses such as *Stipa tenuissima* fit the bill perfectly, as do perennials such as helianthus, rudbeckia, sedum, and eupatorium.

In this garden Bulaitis has used large quantities of one of her favourite grasses, the fine feather grass *Stipa tenuissima,* together with the spiky blue grass *Festuca glauca,* allowing them to tumble over the edges of the stream and the sunray tentacles. The designer gave structure to the planting by using the spiky blue sea holly *Eryngium giganteum* and tall, feathery clumps of fennel alongside airy spikes of *Verbena bonariensis.* By introducing a large number of plants that are loose and languid in form and structure and selecting for the hard landscaping a material that can be sculptred into organic form, she has created a garden in which the conventional distinction between hard and soft landscaping is blurred.

ECHO PARK GARDEN

aNDY cAO

The idea of a garden created from fragments of glass might seem unlikely and even dangerous. That such a garden exists and that the result is a soft and sensuous landscape is a credit to the vision of Andy Cao, its young Vietnamese-American designer. He saw the landscape potential of a material he discovered by chance, and drew his inspiration from a world far removed from the American suburban garden.

After qualifying as a landscape architect, Cao stumbled upon the notion of making a garden with glass when he helped a sculptor friend to create an art installation that used the material. This introduction to glass as a sculptural medium inspired him to find out more about it and a subsequent visit to a glass-recycling plant in California gave him an idea. During the recycling process there is a point at which the glass has been crushed and tumbled to remove any sharp edges but has not yet been melted down. The pieces of glass have a frosty appearance and are safe to hold in the hand. Supplied with a crate load of this material, Cao started to experiment in a landscape context with the glass nuggets, which measure some 12–15cm (5–6in) in diameter, and a highly inventive use of a recycled material was born: the glass garden.

Cao created the first glass garden in his own backyard in Los Angeles. This urban space is ordinary, of modest size, and situated on top of a hill. The far from ordinary garden begins at the side gate, from which a path leads along the side of the house. This is not a conventional path. Instead of the customary gravel, it consists of brown-glass chippings that crunch under foot. As it continues it sweeps between mounds of yellow and green glass and beside a dividing wall made from concrete blocks. This material is disguised with a layer of blue-green and brown-green glass mixed with cement. Most apparent in this area at the side of the house is the lack of a defining line between path and planted areas. There are no identifiable paths or beds; instead the glass surface simply changes colour or rises and falls to suggest a

right *Conical mounds of white glass, resembling piles of salt, emerge from a still pool to form one of the most arresting sights in this unusual creation. Formal and less colourful than the rest of the garden, this feature provides a peaceful place for reflection.*

walkway. A planting of lemon grass emerges from an equally undefined area. Even the nearby wall appears as simply a vertical extension of the ground surface.

Glass pervades the whole garden, unifying horizontal and vertical surfaces. The fact that it can provide both firm surfaces to walk on and a satisfactory mulch means that the traditional distinction between hard and soft landscaping, between paved and planted areas, can be dispensed with. Both dissolve into one soft landscape. Furthermore, unlike materials conventionally used in hard landscaping, glass provides the bonus of colour. It is a substitute for the plants when these are not in flower, and complements them when they are.

Cao's inspiration for the garden was the landscape of his homeland, Vietnam, and this is a garden full of memories. The first is encountered in the side passage, where the banks of coloured glass ranging in hue from yellow to green are a fond reference to the Vietnamese farming practice of piling up rice near the road after the harvest.

In the rear garden another recollected image, of piles of salt being left to dry, inspired the site's most dramatic feature. A group of white conical mounds of glass sits in a still, rectangular pool. The edge of the pool is constructed from black cement and glass and is intended to resemble a mud bank. The stark simplicity of

left *Andy Cao's illustrated plan for the garden shows a design based loosely on a map of Vietnam, with its long, north–south orientation. As a series of interconnected ideas, the design is not restrained by the shape of the plot. Only the pool, in the rear garden, by virtue of its size and rectangular shape, makes any reference to the house. The images that surround the plan provide obvious clues to the inspirations for many of the forms in the garden.*

right *In this detail of the side passage the painterly quality of the garden is evident. The texture of the glass on the ground and on the wall, and the subtle mixing of fragments of coloured glass, are reminiscent of a canvas by the French pointillist Georges Seurat, in which the painter built up images by using dots of pure colour.*

the glass-and-water garden provides a powerful and memorable spectacle, full of energy yet calming. The Vietnamese imagery is completed by the suggestion of a rice field. Feather grass, *Stipa tenuissima*, is planted in rows and resembles rice as it stands in its expanse of blue glass. In this "paddy field" is a sculpture of scrap iron chosen to evoke the military hardware left abandoned in the Vietnamese countryside.

This is not a functional garden, for there are no clearly defined areas such as a patio or lawn for recreation or play. Neither is it intended to be seen as an extension of the house. Its plan is based on a map of Vietnam and makes only a passing reference to the building; the design simply contracts and expands according to the confines of the site. Rather this is a garden of visual symbols or metaphors that have meaning and evoke memories. It is designed to tell the story of a distant time and a distant place, its primary function more like that of a narrative painting, but a three-dimensional one that you can walk around

and experience. The glass acts like a pigment or paint and is the medium that conveys this reflective theme.

Maintenance of the garden consists simply of raking the glass. In the planted areas the material provides similar benefits to those of a gravel mulch. A mulch is a surface dressing that is distributed over the soil. By helping to conserve moisture, repel slugs, and prevent weeds, it reduces the amount of work a garden needs. In this garden some plants, such as bamboos and succulents, benefit from the glass, while others can be scorched by the harsh reflections it creates. In northern climates, light and warmth reflected from glass would be advantageous to all plants.

The planting of the garden is designed to emphasize the irregular and colourful glass surface. To this end, most of the plants were selected for their sculptural look and many are succulents with soft, fleshy foliage. Judicious pruning regulates their size and shape to maintain maximum impact. The choice of plants, which includes agaves, with their distinctive, sword-like

leaves, and colourful flowering kalanchoes, is complemented by the equally colourful nuggets of glass mulch.

Like colours on an artist's palette, the pieces of glass are mixed painstakingly. One colour alone would not have the desired three-dimensional qualities. There are no hard edges; surfaces and forms merge into one another in a fusion of light and colour to create a glittering Abstract-Expressionist vision.

Despite the crunchy texture of the material, the overall impression is one of luxuriant softness. Never has an industrial material been made to look so organic and sensuous. The properties of glass cause it to change appearance in response to time and weather. It is Cao's discovery of the potential of glass in the garden that is so original. Even if one fails to recognize his symbolic references to Vietnam, this garden still shows the value of investigating and experimenting with new and unconventional materials. Here the result was the discovery of an alternative mulch. Most conventional mulches are drab in colour and discreet, but Cao's inspired introduction of a multicoloured glass equivalent, one that can also be mounded and sculpted, has radically transformed an unexceptional urban plot.

It is hard to find precedents, historical or otherwise, for a garden such as this. To the best of my knowledge, glass in this recycled form has never before been used in a garden. Glass marbles have been employed as a mulch but because they are expensive in any quantity they have not been favoured by many designers. Furthermore they are unsuitable for paths and are not as versatile as Cao's discovery.

When raked, the glass surface might suggest a Japanese Zen garden, but the resemblance ends there. The vivid colours, sparkling effects, and multiplicity of forms are not restrained and do not invite quiet contemplation (although the pool area is well suited to this). In eighteenth-century Europe polychromatic stones and gravels were used instead of carpet bedding to create parterres with complex patterns, but Cao's garden has little to do with the European heritage either. What makes this glass garden different is as much to do with his Vietnamese cultural roots. It is they that have protected him from the straitjacket of traditional Western garden design and allowed him to approach this project in such a fresh and original way.

above *Along the side passage concrete flagstones give way to an informal path defined only by the use of different-coloured glass fragments and sculptured mounds of glass. Lemon grass lines the path and bananas grow along the top of the garden's boundary wall, which is made from concrete blocks covered with coloured glass mixed with cement.*

right *Strong contrasts of both form and texture abound in this garden. Here the spiky yet smooth and succulent forms of agave plants, growing in a bed of crushed blue glass, are seen beyond the softer, finely textured forms of the conical mounds of white glass that sit in a mirror-like pool. Sited in the rear garden, the pool provides an area for quiet contemplation.*

THE RITENOUR GARDEN

mIA lEHRER

Designed for a jazz guitarist and his wife, this contemporary garden on a sloping site in Malibu, California, is based on musical improvisation. The brief included a swimming pool and a terrace, but the local building code dictated that a large part of the garden had to be constructed in permeable materials. The result is a series of jazz-inspired essays that contrast soft and hard landscaping.

A large feature such as a swimming pool can dominate a garden and can easily appear to be more part of the architecture than of the landscape. The American landscape designer Thomas Church solved the problem by revising the shape of the pool, in many cases giving it an organic shape inspired by the local landscape. Others have sought to disguise the feature by making it seem like part of the natural terrain.

Similarly, a hard-surfaced terrace, usually placed close to the house for convenience, can seem detached from a planted garden when the two meet abruptly. In the past the formal style of garden design solved this problem by extending the architecture into the garden. The English landscape style allowed the landscape to come right up to the house. In the *Ritenour Garden*

Mia Lehrer achieves an unusual compromise. The pool and terrace are cleverly integrated with, and not separated from, the soft landscaping. Both hard and soft landscaping adjoin the house.

The standard rectangular swimming pool is given interest by the wave pattern created by tiles of different shades of blue on its sides and bottom. This pattern is continued in the large area of grass which surrounds the pool and which constitutes the major part of the pool garden replacing the customary large area of paving. The striped-lawn effect is created by the use of two different species of grass.

Steps lead down from the upper swimming-pool area. Formed in concrete for practical reasons, they are softened by their curving shape, which mirrors the wave pattern of the lawn. A thin

right The wave pattern created in blue tiles in the swimming pool is subtly extended into the surrounding lawn by the use of two different kinds of grass. The same wave shape is used to soften the concrete steps that lead down to the terrace.

right The plan of the garden shows a quite structured organization of the different elements, which include a swimming pool, terrace, and tennis court. On closer inspection, however, the fluidity of this design becomes apparent. Hard and soft landscaping merge into each other, softening edges and unifying the garden.

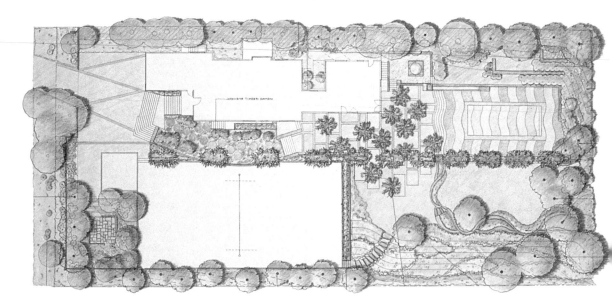

left *In a witty design idea, based on role reversal, islands of grass provide soft stepping stones across a sea of black, rounded pebbles. The darkness of the pebbles contrasts with the foliage and the stems of the bamboos.*

right *With its mixture of coloured slabs of concrete, grass dividing strips, and towering palms, the terrace conveys a sense of informality. At the same time the designer has respected the practical necessity of providing a hard surface close to the house.*

strip of grass between the treads and risers further softens the steps and introduces the idea of soft and hard landscaping as integrated and inseparable, which is continued on the terrace.

On the terrace is an improvised pattern of rectangular, coloured concrete pads, some tinted to match the walls of the house, kept apart, or perhaps held together, by strips of grass. From some of these turfed areas a variety of palm trees emerge. The two ingredients, soft grass and solid concrete, reach the house together in one direction and spread out into the rest of the garden in the other. Farther along the terrace, where firm surfaces are not required, the final essay in hard and soft is presented. In

a reversal of roles the concrete pads are replaced with stepping-stone-like circles of grass. Intended to appear like a series of musical notes, these sit in a sea of rounded dark pebbles that laps up to the house and spreads right across the terrace.

At first this garden appears to be of a modern but conventional design. Closer examination reveals an ingenious solution to the problem of maintaining the greenery of soft landscaping when major architectural features such as a swimming pool or terrace are called for. The formal and the informal are integrated, not separated, in a garden which in plan seems structured but is in fact of a loose design. Here hard and soft share the same space.

AILLEURS

pHILIPPE nIGRO & cLAIRE gARDET

Two imaginative French art students, with no training or experience in garden design, have adopted an unlikely material and means of construction to make a garden that is not only soft and sensuous but also portable.

The Festival International des Jardins has taken place each year since 1992 at the Château de Chaumont-sur-Loire in France. Created in the "English style" in the nineteenth century, the landscaped gardens of the château provide an unlikely romantic setting for a festival that is dedicated to encouraging a contemporary and an experimental approach to garden design. Within the grounds an area of about three hectares (7½ acres) has been given over permanently to the festival. The Belgian designer Jacques Wirtz devised the layout for the exhibits, specifying thirty individual spaces, each of about 250 sq m (2700 sq ft), and each enclosed by a beech hedge. All are rectangular, but their rear boundaries and both sides curve inwards, and each garden has a single access point at the front. This arrangement is unlike that of most garden and flower shows, where the plots allocated for gardens are never identical and the public are rarely allowed to enter the gardens themselves. The standardization of the exhibition areas removes any hint of exclusivity. This democratic approach is reinforced by a stipulation that every garden must be achievable within a fixed budget that is the same for each. Given also the fact that each year a theme is set for the designers, the results provide an informative exhibition where visitors can easily compare like with like.

In order to encourage experimentation and diversity, the organizers often look beyond the disciplines of landscape and garden design for contributors. By inviting designers or artists whose work is not directly linked with landscape design they aim to promote fresh ideas free of traditional preconceptions or standard references. In keeping with this principle, the organizers of the 1996 event invited the students of the nearby Ecole Boulle to submit a project. From the school's many submissions a selection panel chose a garden called *Ailleurs (Elsewhere)*.

Were it not for the handful of plants dotted about, it would be easy to dismiss this creation as having very little to do with garden design. The winners, art students Philippe Nigro and Claire Gardet, have displayed a creditable lack of inhibition in arriving at their own definition of the garden. Embracing modern sculpture and installation art, their design offers a strongly three-dimensional interpretation of the space. They have created an environment that is more about presenting an experience than producing a space for cultivation or other pastimes normally associated with the garden. The project is a refreshing example of returning to first principles since it has rejected most of the elements of the standard model for garden design.

A screen of dense mixed vegetation conceals the garden at the front and from the main thoroughfare that connects all the gardens. This, coupled with the beech hedges that surround the permanent site, has created a garden that, from the outside, is almost completely enclosed and invisible. The only access into the garden is through a gap in the middle of the planting at the front, where there is a small wooden tunnel. A wooden walkway leads the visitor through the tunnel into a bright-red world created by huge expanses of heavy-duty canvas stretched between wooden posts. At night in particular, walking into the garden, with its colourful, soft, curving, suspended canvas forms, must have conjured up for some visitors memories of entering a "Big Top" circus tent. The strong and weatherproof tent fabric has been machined to create the desired shapes, which are supplied in many places with rigid, circular apertures through which timber poles project. Fixed to these poles by chains, the canvas is supported off the ground. The combination of upright poles and shaped canvas creates a sculptured, surreal landscape of rising and dipping surfaces and a skyline of peaks and troughs.

below *A variegated phormium and a cactus emerge from this bright-red, undulating landscape. A wooden walkway provides access around a garden which, because it is made and erected like a tent, could provide the answer for those in search of an imaginative portable garden.*

Although the soft canvas surfaces seem designed to tempt one to leap up on to them, like an adult "bouncy castle," they are not meant to be encroached upon, and a small rope barrier runs along the full length of the walkway, which is made of wooden decking. This walkway begins at the entrance, providing the only legitimate pathway through and around the garden.

Planting in the garden is minimal, restricted to a small number of feature shrubs, trees, and cacti. Each has been chosen for its distinctive and contrasting character. In this garden organic matter replaces the usual statuary as the ornamental detail. The selection includes *Agave americana*, *Buxus sempervirens*, *Cereus uruguayanus* 'Monstruosus', *Ficus benjamina*, and *Yucca gloriosa*. The plants are like living sculptures in a garden in which ground cover is not provided by vegetation but by contoured canvas.

Positioned close to the walkway on the lower slopes of the structure, they emerge through circular apertures in the canvas floor. It is no coincidence that all the plants selected have green foliage of one shade or another. No other colour of plant foliage or flower is used. Green was regarded by the designers as the best colour to complement the red of the background and to make the plants stand out.

If one were to assess this exhibit in terms of the space it provides for activities such as gardening or play, it would fail miserably. If instead one considered what function this idea might serve or where it could be used, then the concept has great potential. What is novel about this garden is that the canvas "tent" completely conceals the ground and is suspended above it. These two attributes make a garden of this type ideal where the

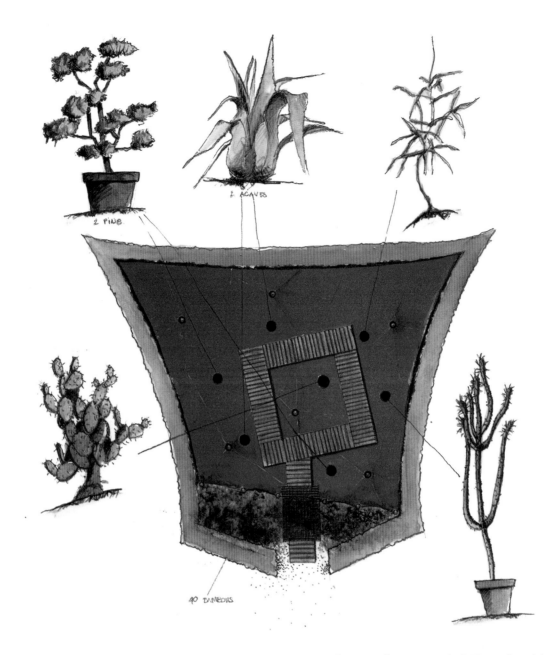

existing ground surface is unattractive or inhospitable for plants. The structure could easily and quickly be erected to hide a hard and ugly concrete floor, and because it is raised off the ground, would allow the introduction of plants in raised containers. By increasing the area of decking and the planting pockets one could create on almost any flat piece of ground an enclosed, soft, and sensuous garden in which to relax and sunbathe. Even an office car park could be converted into a pleasant place in which to spend the lunch hour in summer.

Since the structure is similar to a marquee, with canvas supported and held taut by timber poles, chains, and guy ropes, the whole garden is by implication extremely portable. Like a circus tent, it can be erected in a short time, and after use it can be as easily dismantled and taken to another location, or stored

in a small space until it is next required. What at first might have seemed eccentric, and perhaps even unusable, has in fact the potential to become a practical portable garden that would be suitable for use outside temporary accommodation. The sloping surfaces could be washed with ease, and if erected above an area of soil, would suppress weed growth by restricting the amount of light reaching the ground.

Canvas, often plastic-coated, and other synthetic fabrics are an established part of the city street, in the form of canopies and awnings for shop fronts and open-air restaurants and bars. Now Nigro and Gardet have introduced canvas into the garden, not to provide shelter or shade but as a way of landscaping the space. It might look like a circus tent or a trampoline, but the overriding impression it gives is of a soft and an inviting landscape.

THE SPIRIT OF THE PLACE

jULIE tOLL, tHOMAS nORDSTRÖM & aNNIKA oSKARSSON

These intriguing "puffing mosses" appear to be natural phenomena sitting in a wild, untended part of the Swedish countryside. But in fact they are the result of a combination of subtle landscaping and technical ingenuity.

This garden was created by the English garden designer Julie Toll, working alongside Swedish craftsmen and sculptors, for an exhibition of gardens and crafts held at the Rosendal Garden near Stockholm in Sweden in 1998. The exhibition, which was part of the city's year-long tenure as the Cultural Capital of Europe, sought to bring together the art and the craft of the garden. It displayed the work of craftsmen within an existing garden and the surrounding landscape, and in addition eleven new concept gardens were created in the exhibition area.

The site for this garden, one of the new creations, was chosen with great care to ensure that it embodied "the spirit of the place. " It consists of a natural, open, sunny clearing on a wooded slope that drops down to a damp, flat area adjoining a meadow.

Julie Toll is well known as a designer who specializes in creating natural gardens using wild flowers. In this garden she has introduced a granite water staircase that descends the slope among existing oak woodland. At the bottom the staircase opens out into a dark, rocky pool surrounded by marginal and bog planting that simply merges with the surrounding meadow land. The garden has no well-defined edges; instead its boundaries are soft, and along their whole length they simply blend into the natural landscape in such a way that it is difficult to see exactly where the garden begins and ends.

Set into the pool is a series of what, to a casual observer, might appear to be natural mossy tussocks, the sort of feature often seen around pools where cattle or sheep come to drink, trampling the boggy margins into humps and hollows as they do so. These mossy humps are, however, man-made and consist of chicken wire moulded into shape and filled with compost on which lush deep moss has been allowed to grow. The humps sit on supports installed in the water and are connected by pipes to a smoke

machine hidden in the nearby undergrowth. The machine is controlled by a random timer, which means that the tussocks suddenly start to puff smoke for no apparent reason. The effect they create varies with the weather – sometimes the smoke rises straight up, while at other times the wind blows it almost horizontally. During still, calm weather a "mist" hangs over the pool even after the smoke machine has switched itself off.

The "puffing mosses" were created by Thomas Nordström and Annika Oskarsson, who had recently finished their training as artists. The pieces are living sculptures in which a mossy exterior has been made to grow over a man-made interior. They could also be described as "soft" sculptures. In the past most outdoor sculpture intended to be permanent was made exclusively of stone, wood, or cast bronze. Recent years have seen the introduction of other materials, such as steel, plastic, and glass, which, like the more traditional materials, provide a robust, hard surface. Here, by contrast, a living material has been used to make a sculpture that is both soft and self-maintaining. Moreover, these pieces belong to their environment in a way that a stone or bronze sculpture never could. This is because they are covered in a natural material and so at first do not appear to be art objects, but simply an extension of their watery environment. It is art joining with nature rather than imposing itself upon it.

Even though an elaborate kinetic trick is involved, the effect of the puffing mosses is so gentle and transient that it blends

right *Smoke, generated by a machine fitted with a timing device, is piped to the mossy tussocks and puffs out at random intervals. Although an artificial and a sophisticated creation, the garden is designed to blend seamlessly into the surrounding landscape. Cultivated non-native plants, such as* Cornus alba 'Spaethii', *to the rear of the pond, sit happily among natural meadow grass.*

perfectly into the natural surroundings. From a distance one could easily mistake the smoke for a cloud of early-morning mist lying in the hollows at the edge of a field. This garden is very much a twentieth-century concept, but the desire for gardens that mimic nature, albeit in a controlled form, has almost certainly existed throughout the history of gardening.

Wild and woodland gardening was an established style as early as medieval times in Europe, and records from that era indicate that informally managed areas were introduced within the fortified walls of castles. In England during the seventeenth and eighteenth centuries the "wilderness" was a popular feature of many grand gardens. The wildness of the English landscape style, with its dense trees and shrubs cut through by a maze of paths, was an idealized version of nature inspired by the imaginary landscapes of the French painters Claude and Poussin. Wild gardening in Britain could be said to have peaked in popularity in the early twentieth century, when it was adopted as an antidote to the excessive formalism of the Victorians. Gardeners such as Gertrude Jekyll and William Robinson promoted the use of plants that were not necessarily native but which were perfectly hardy and required little maintenance. The introduction of many new plants, particularly from China and the Himalayas, at the end of the nineteenth century and the beginning of the twentieth, gave these gardeners a wealth of new material with which to create their naturalistic woodlands.

In all these historical styles informality, and even wildness, was defined and confined by the introduction of structure or barriers.

The hand of the designer was always in evidence, most notably in the use of imported plants. Julie Toll's idea was to develop this garden "as found." In many ways her approach is as radical as the Dada artists' use of found or ready-made objects as sculpture. But the visual result of her interpretation was unlikely to be greeted by the outrage that the Dadaists provoked. In this wild garden she has made full use of the existing natural flora. Oak woodland is particularly well suited to the introduction of new planting as the trees have deep roots and a relatively open canopy that does not smother underplanting. Also, because oaks are very long-lived, they are ideal for the establishment of a long-term garden. The area that surrounds the pool containing the puffing mosses consists of a well-crafted mix of indigenous grasses and introduced bog and marginal plants. The non-indigenous species provide a variety of colours and textures.

Apart, of course, from its inventive use of modern technology, what most distinguishes this style of garden from its historical precedents is its lack of boundaries. It was designed not only to look entirely natural but also to join seamlessly with the countryside all about it. There is minimal structure and even the rocky waterfall melts into its surroundings with little evidence of human intervention. It is this absence of apparent order, with no sign of the designer's touch, that gives the garden its softness. This is a place of sensations to be experienced rather than one to be intellectually understood. Because this is a show garden it does not have to relate to an adjacent property. A domestic garden so free of boundaries is a very rare occurrence.

below *A low, rustic wooden rail is the only boundary to be found anywhere in this garden. To the rear the margins of the pool simply merge with the edge of a field of flax. Around the water's edge bog plants have been introduced to provide colour and texture. Among those selected are astilbes, bergamot, candelabra primulas, and Ligularia 'The Rocket'. No more than a slight breeze is needed to make the smoke from the puffing mosses swirl and eddy above the pool, where it hangs like an early-morning mist.*

PAUL COOPER GARDEN

NIGHT GARDEN

pAUL cOOPER

The author of this book used materials and techniques associated with the theatre to provide busy clients with a garden that comes into its own when night falls and most other gardens have gone to sleep.

Not long before I met the clients, their London house had been extended to include a new conservatory of a Minimalist design, with a plain-glass wall from roof to floor and an all-glass roof supported on glass trusses. The new room enlarged the living space, but the garden did not do justice to it. A closer view of a neglected garden was not what the owners had intended.

The plot was slightly longer than the typical garden of a British semi-detached house. Like many urban gardens, it posed various problems. It was dominated by a number of large trees, both within the garden and in those on either side. These not only took sustenance from potential planting areas but in summer also left most of the garden with little or no direct light. Since most of them were deciduous, in winter their leafless skeletons added to the garden's bleak aspect. The trees, however, had to be retained, either because they were subject to preservation orders or because the neighbours wished to retain theirs. Moreover, the garden faced north, so the three-storeyed house created additional shade, especially near the conservatory.

The owners, preferring the restrained, geometric, and unfussy forms of modern architecture to anything old-fashioned wanted a correspondingly formal garden. They also wanted a garden that could provide visual interest all year round and, they emphasized, one that would look good even at night. Both husband and wife worked long hours and for much of the year rarely saw the

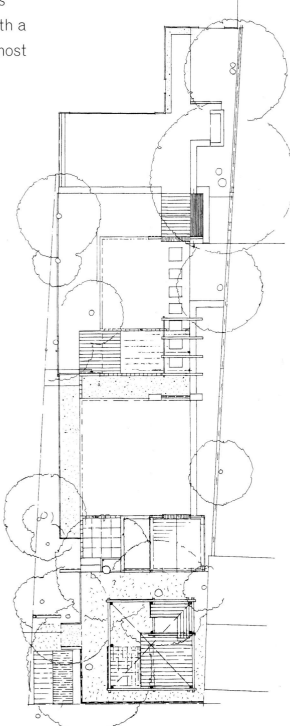

right *The plan shows a geometric, formal, and not unconventional scheme, based on a series of rectangles and squares. This solution was devised in response to the clients' desire for a garden that was Modernist rather than traditional or retrospective.*

garden in daylight. They also wanted to have something to look out at when they used the conservatory on winter evenings.

In plan the garden is based around two squares separated by a rectangular formal pool. The first square, the more shaded, is planted with a strongly growing woodland grass which would allow spring bulbs to be naturalized among it. This grassy area is surrounded on two sides by a sea of shade-tolerant ground-cover planting. On the west side of the garden a neat row of stepping stones leads from the house through the square of grass and across the pool, under a cantilevered pergola. Along this side of the garden a low retaining wall, painted white to match the house, has been built to provide a raised planting bed, free from the roots of the trees and in the sunnier part of the plot. This and another planter at the rear of the garden are the only areas capable of sustaining a wide variety of shrubs and herbaceous plants. The second square, blessed with sunshine, is simply a clearly defined lawn and provides a sense of space in what is otherwise a confined garden. Facing this lawn and southwards towards the house, there is an additional hard sitting area with a tent-like collapsible summer house beside it. This is one of the few places in the garden where one can sit and enjoy the sunshine.

The elements that are intended to transform this garden exploit not the horizontal plane, but the vertical. Here a touch of theatricality has been introduced. Placed strategically about the garden are simple tall, white, rectangular frames. A screen made from the back-projection material used in stage design can be inserted in each one. By day the light-sensitive screens bounce additional natural light into the gloomy garden and break it up into a series of "rooms," hiding some of it from view and adding a sense of mystery.

But it is at night that they begin to perform their principal task. A combination of concealed lighting and projectors turns the screens into walls of illuminated single colour or spectacular images. These remote-controlled devices provide an entertaining light show that brings the garden alive at night. Visible from the conservatory, the spectacle can even be enjoyed in the depths of winter, when the garden is at its dullest. When silhouetted against a single blue- or red-lit screen, even the leafless and lifeless-looking trees are interesting, their shapes and forms becoming

right *It is when darkness falls that this garden fully reveals its innovative nature. Projectors and concealed light sources bring to life a series of screens made from back-projection material. Positioned at key points within the garden, these create the required mood as well as giving shape, form, and colour to the space.*

left *All kinds of images can be projected onto the screens from behind or in front. Here colourful abstract shapes provide interest, but pictures of plants and gardens could also be displayed in order to create the illusion of a garden within a garden.*

below *On a winter night a free-standing screen bathed in red light from a programmed projector silhouettes a leafless deciduous tree, transforming it into an intriguing image with a strong shape and line.*

almost sculptural. Changing the projected colours changes the mood of the garden – blue might be used for a warm summer evening, red for a cool winter night, perhaps. In summer the white projection screens can be removed to give a wider view of the garden, and reinstalled for a barbecue or party.

One could even project a picture of a completely different garden, making it possible to admire, say, the springtime splendours of a Gertrude Jeykll-inspired herbaceous border on a midwinter evening. One might call this a Jekyll and Hyde garden. By day it is an unassuming, rather formal garden, but after dark it takes on a quite different guise. Only then is its true role as a garden of the night revealed.

Since moving into garden design from a career in sculpture in the mid-1980s I have questioned the traditional definition of a garden. I have asked what a garden is and what it is for. I have challenged the way we make gardens, believing it possible to design them to be more in tune with the demands of modern life. To this end I have introduced new, previously ignored, materials, some to provide immediate solutions, others simply to allow more flexibility. In this project the use of a material not normally found in the garden made it possible to enjoy the space at night.

The project also illustrates a direction that I have been eager to pursue, in which the garden is considered as a stage set. Each garden provides the setting for an imaginary play, in keeping with the owner's interests and lifestyle. In this way the garden has meaning for the client and encourages him or her to engage in its development. I do not regard a garden at any time as a finished entity but as something that should evolve and be adaptable to the changing demands of those who use it.

DIRECTORY OF MATERIALS

Alternative planting mediums It is possible to grow plants in planting mediums other than soil. Inert inorganic materials such as mineral wool provide a rooting medium through which a solution of nutrients is circulated. This form of cultivation is ideal where it is necessary to keep a crop clean or where soil-borne pests and diseases are a problem.

Back-projection screens Made from sheet vinyl stretched over a frame and used with one or more projectors and garden lighting, back-projection screens can bring a sense of theatre to the garden.

Fabrics Modern weatherproof and water-resistant synthetic fabrics are suitable for outdoor use. Canvas-like acrylic textiles are an alternative to cotton and are available in many colours. PVC fabric is made from polyvinyl chloride, a tough, transparent, solid polymer that is easily coloured. Acrylic textiles and PVC fabrics can make weather-resistant canopies and screens or outdoor scatter cushions. Open-weave man-made fabrics are an alternative to solid fencing.

Galvanized metal Iron coated with zinc to protect it against rust is known as galvanized metal. In sheet form, flat or corrugated, it is shiny, with a mottled surface. It can be used to make planters and as a walling material. Although it can retain its reflective appearance for many years, unlike stainless steel it eventually becomes dull and grey. It is also less durable than stainless steel.

Glass Can be used in the garden as a screen to protect against the weather without spoiling a view. Semi-opaque glass provides privacy. Glass can also be used as a flooring material, providing an alternative to wooden decking when an elevated platform is required. It has the added benefit of allowing light to pass through it onto planting or windows below it. When it is used as a vertical surface, its reflective properties create intriguing optical illusions. Strengthened clear or translucent glass can be used vertically or as flooring, but it should be installed by a specialist. Translucent glass is made by acid-etching the surface or by sandblasting; the latter provides a non-slip surface. Glass nuggets and recycled bottle glass make a colourful mulch.

Lighting Fibre-optic and low-voltage lighting systems can extend the use of the garden at night and can also create an extensive range of visual effects.

Mirrors A mirror can give the illusion of depth in a garden. Large glass mirrors are expensive and difficult to handle, and "metallized" plastic-laminate mirrors are a more practical alternative. The reflected image provided by a plastic-laminate mirror is not as good as that from a glass mirror, but it is acceptable in a garden. The material is also easier and safer to use than glass.

Paints Vinyl-based emulsion paints, which are water soluble, can be used to colour most porous surfaces and many are designed to withstand the weather.

They can enliven a dull wall and create a colourful backdrop for planting. It is even possible to paint a rockery.

Plexiglas Known in the UK as Perspex, Plexiglas is a tough, light acrylic thermoplastic used instead of glass. It comes in transparent, translucent, or opaque forms and a range of colours. Easier and safer to use than glass, it can be cut and drilled with DIY tools. In the garden it can be used as a screen or, with a timber or steel frame, as roofing material. Coloured transparent and translucent kinds can be used like stained glass to create daytime light effects.

Rubber and plastic Some types of rubber flooring will survive outdoors but many deteriorate rapidly. Rigid rubber tiles are not suitable as they are not colour-fast and are likely to become slippery. Softer, absorbent, heavy-duty types of rubber flooring are more reliable. Plastic (vinyl) flooring is flexible and durable, but strong colours may fade in bright sunlight. All rubber and plastic flooring should be laid on a firm base, such as concrete.

Stainless steel Tarnish- and rust-resistant, stainless steel can be polished to an almost mirror-like finish and can even be coloured by a process involving the interference of light with its passive oxide layer. All the colours of the spectrum can be created and the results are colour-fast. Stainless steel in sheet form is ideal for containers and vertical surfaces where a durable, low-maintenance, highly reflective, and high tech finish is desired.

Steel In tubular or other sections, steel is slender and strong and can be used to create elegant and dynamic structures. It can give a contemporary look to traditional garden features such as gazebos and pergolas. Ordinary mild steel can be prevented from rusting by the application of appropriate protective paint.

Wood Softwoods, pressure-treated with preservatives, have reduced the need to use hardwoods from tropical forests. Their use for planters, trellis screens, frames for climbing plants, and other structures has been revolutionized by multicoloured water-based wood stains. Wooden decking is popular in modern gardens, and hardwoods such as oak are best for it as they need no surface protection or treatment and are hard-wearing and long-lasting. Exterior-grade plywood is a resin-bonded wood laminate which is very strong and can be used as a wall material as well as to make planters and other garden features.

Wood treatments Brush-applied wood preservatives treat only the surface of wood and must be applied regularly. They are not a substitute for pressure-treated wood when there is prolonged contact with the ground. There are two types of wood stain. Most solvent-based stains contain wood preservative. They are toxic when wet and retain some toxicity when dry. Water-based stains are safer to use, but most only colour wood and few also protect it.

INDEX

Page numbers in *italics* refer to captions/ illustrations alone

A

Abstraction 82
"Ailleurs" 176–9
Alberti, Leon Battista 108, 120–2
Alexandre, Joelle 144–7
alternative planting mediums 144, 146
American gardens 14–15, *17*, 38–41, 50–3, 76–9, 109–10, 116–23, 130–3, 140, 141–3, 152–5, 160, 162–75
"An Idea" 86–9
Arp, Jean 160
Art Nouveau 10
artificiality 21, 50–3, 100, *101*, 142, 152, 154, 155
Arts and Crafts Movement 9
"Atlantis Mariposa" 32–7
Ault, Emily 46–9

B

back-projection screens 186–8
Balston, Michael 70–5
Barnett, Rod 124–9
Baroque style 13
Barragán, Luis 40, 41, 124
Barron, William *10*, 13
Batter Kay Associates 130–3
Bernini, Gianlorenzo 84
"Blue Garden, The" 28–31
Bradley-Hole, Christopher *19*, 24–7
Bramante, Donato 108
Brookes, John 15, 72
Brown, Barbara *83*
Brown, "Capability" 140
Browne, Enrique 110
Bulaitis, Bonita *4*, *5*, 16, 148–51, *157*, 162–5
Burton, Decimus *9*

C

Calder, Alexander 82, *84*
Cao, Andy 160, 166–71
Cardasis, Dean 55, 76–9
ceramics 10, *11*, *152–3*, 154
Chaumont-sur-Loire Festival gardens 86–9,
142, 144–7, 176–9
Chelsea Flower Show gardens 24–7, *58*, 59, 70–5, 142
Chermayeff, Serge 15
Chinese gardens 16, 21
Christo 159, *160–1*
Church, Thomas *12*, 14–15, 172
Claude 182
concrete 12, 38, 40, *41*, *62*, 64, 127, 150, 152, 160, 175
Conran, Terence 148
conservatories 9, *72*, 109, 112–15, 185–6
Constructivism 12, *14*, 45, 82
Cooper, Paul (garden) 184–8
cottage gardens 10, 12, *70–1*, *74–5*
Cubism 82

D

Dadaism 16, 20, *23*, 44, 159, 182
Dali, Salvador 22, 159
de Maria, Walter 22
decking 14, 24, *26–7*, *68*, 76, 98, *99*, *100*, *134*, 144–6, *146–7*, 148, *148–9*, 176, *176–7*, 178
Delaney, Topher 20, 38–41
Denise, Jean-Christophe 86–9
Donnell Garden, Sonoma *12*
Duchamp, Marcel 20, 44, 45
Dupont-Rougier, Vincent 144–7

E

"Echo Park Garden" 166–71
Eckbo, Garrett 14
Egyptian gardens 64
Ehrlich, Steven 110
Eighteenth-century gardens 12, 15, 38, 108, 118, 124, 140, 182
Elvaston Castle, Derbyshire *10*, 13
English gardens 9–10, 13, 16, 46–9, 94–7, 108, *110*, 112–15, 118, 124, 134–7, 140, 150, 176, 182, 184–8

F

fabrics, synthetic 8, 70, *70–1*, *72–3*, 75, 148, *148–9*, *150–1*, 158–60, *160–1*, 176–9
Festival International des Jardins

see Chaumont-sur-Loire
Fish Bros 46–8
Flavin, Dan 104
flooring 46, 59, 150, 155, 160
see also stone: paving
Fogg, Julia 148–51
Fountain Plaza, Dallas 17
fountains 8, 13, 15, *17*, 40, *75*, *82*, 83–5, 86–9, 133
French gardens *8*, 13, 15, *17*, *50*, 52, *52–3*, 84, 143, 150, 176
"Fuller House, The" 116–19

G

Gabo, Naum 12, *14*, 82
"Garden and Conservatory" 112–15
Gardet, Claire 176–9
Gaudí, Antonio *6*, 10, *11*, 64
"Gibbs Garden, The" 124–9
glass 8, 12, 24, *25*, *27*, *29*, 30, 36, 38, 40, 72, *74–5*, 94–6, *97*, 109, 112–15, 148–50, *150–1*, 160, 166–71, 180
see also conservatories; mirrors
Gold-Friedman residence *110*
Goldsworthy, Andy *21*, 22
granite *see* stone
Gropius, Walter 12, 14
"Growing Vision" 148–51
Gutbrod, Rolf 65

H

Halland, Sussex 15
Hampton Court, London 72
  Flower Show gardens 28–31, 143, 148–51
hanging garden, Santiago 110, *111*
Haussmann, Georges 63
Hellerup, Copenhagen 15
Hicks, Ivan 22, *23*
High Tech 9, *14*, 54–79
Huidobro, Borja 110, *110–11*

I, J

instantaneity 10, 13, 72, 138–55
Italian gardens 12, 13, 22, 75, *82*, 83, 84–5, 108, 120–2, 124, 127, 130–3, 150
Jacobsen, Arne 159
Jacobsen, Preben 72

Japanese gardens 8, 20, *50–1*, 52, *53*, 90–3, 98–101, 128
Jeanne-Claude 159, *160–1*
Jekyll, Gertrude 9–10, 12, *70–1*, *74–5*, 182, 188
Jones, Jenny 94–7
"Just What Is It" *158*

K, L

Kew Gardens, London 9
Kiley, Dan Urban 14, 15, *17*
"Kuhling Garden, The" 38–41
Kukorelli, Peter *140–1*
Kuramata, Shiro 56
landscape gardening 15, 22, 108, 118, 124, 140, 142–3, 152–5, 160, 182
  see also eighteenth-century gardens
Le Corbusier 56, 109
Le Nôtre, André *8*, 13, 15
Lehrer, Mia 160, 172–5
lighting 41, 48, *58*, 59, 85, *110*, 162
  fibre-optic 38, *39*, 104
  laser 104
  neon 102–5
  shows 186–8
  solar-powered 100, *101*, 142, *142–3*
Lightning Field, New Mexico 22
"Littman Wedding Garden, The" *139*, 152–5
"Living Sculpture" *19*, 24–7
Loudon, J.C. 60–3
Lutyens, Edwin 9–10, 12

M

McLaughlin, Niall 134–7
Mannerism 22, *82*, 84–5
Marx, Roberto Burle *15*, 160
Masuno, Shunmyo 90–3
medieval gardens 84, 182
metals 8, 12, 41, 42, *42–3*, 44–5, 46, 64, 72–4, 96, 134, 162, *162–3*, 165
  galvanized 24, *25*, 114, *114–15*, *130–1*, 133
  see also steel
Millennium Dome, London 110
mineral wool 144, 146
Minimalism *19*, 24–7, *102–3*, 128, 185
Miró, Joan 160

mirrors 46–7, 48, 59, 114, 114–15, 122, 122–3, 142
Modernism 16, 17, 35, 68, 127, 128, 140, 148
Moholy-Nagy, Laszlo 82
Molta, Liliana 86–9
"Moving Garden, The" 140–1
Müller, Hans-Jürgen and Helga 32–7

N, O
Nadeau, Patrick 144–7
Nakaya, Fujiko 63, 65
"Napa Valley Retreat" 130–3
Neo-Constructivism 16–17
Neutra, Richard 109
"Night Garden" 184–8
Nigro, Philippe 176–9
Nineteenth-century gardens 9–10, 13, 38, 112, 118, 134, 176, 182
"Nomadic Vegetable Garden, The" 144–7
Nordstrom, Thomas 180–3
"Odenwald Garden" 42–5
Oehme, Wolfgang 165
Office Garden 22, 23
Op Art 82–3
Oppenheim, Meret 159
Oskarsson, Annika 180–3
Otto, Frei 65

P
paint 20, 21, 29, 30, 31, 38, 40, 41, 42–3, 44, 50–1, 52, 52–3, 152, 152–3, 154, 154–5, 155
Parc de la Villette, Paris 10, 16
parks, public 60–5
Parque Güell, Barcelona 6, 10, 11, 64
Paxton, Joseph 9, 63
Pearson, Dan 58, 59, 110
Persian gardens 21, 27, 124
Perspex see Plexiglas
Pevsner, Antoine 12
"Photographer's Retreat, A" 134–7
Piazza Navona, Rome 84
"Plastic Garden, The" 55, 76–9
plastics 8, 14, 46, 47, 50–1, 52–3, 86–9, 144, 144–5, 146, 180
    flooring 160

lights 58, 59
    thermoplastics 158
Plaza de la Fuentes, Mexico City 124
Plaza del Bebedero, Mexico City 124
"Plaza of Whiteness" 90–3
Plexiglas 12, 14, 76–8, 79
Pointillism 168
pottery see ceramics
Poussin, Nicolas 182
Predock, Antoine 107, 110, 116–23
"Puffing Mosses" 180–3

R
"Reflective Garden, A" 70–5
Renaissance gardens 50, 52, 52–3, 83–4, 108, 120–2, 124, 127
Revolver Creek, South Africa 20, 21
Riley, Bridget 83
"Ritenour Garden, The" 172–5
Robinson, William 182
Rococo Wood 141–2
Rogers, Richard 14, 56
Roman gardens 83, 124, 130–3
Romaniuk, Peter 112–15
Rose, James 14, 78
Rosendal exhibition garden 180–3
"Row Housing" 66–9
rubber 47, 59, 86, 155, 160
Ryoan-ji 20

S
Santer, Susan 148–51
Schaudt Architekten 66–9
Schwartz, Martha 50–3, 85, 139, 142–3, 152–5, 160
Scrupe, Mara Adamitz 141–2, 142–3
seating, Commerce 160
Seurat, Georges 168
Seventeenth-century gardens 8, 13, 15, 17, 64, 72, 84, 108, 143, 182
"Showa Memorial Park" 60–5
Simon, Jacques 22
Sixteenth-century gardens 22, 64, 82, 84–5, 108, 127
Smyth, Ted 102–5
Sorenson, Carl 15
Speckhardt, Ri and Siegfried 42–5

"Splice Garden, The" 50–3
steel 10, 12, 16, 22, 24, 30, 31, 50, 52, 52–3, 64–5, 65, 68, 69, 72, 109, 110, 112, 114, 120–1, 122, 128, 130–1, 133, 148, 148–9, 180
    sculptures 42–3, 44, 57, 102–3, 104
    stainless 57, 59, 68, 70, 70–1, 72–5, 94, 96, 144
"Spirit of the Place, The" 180–3
Stevens, David 28–31, 57
stone 20, 21, 24, 30, 31, 35, 36–7, 40, 41, 42–3, 68, 69, 90–3, 116, 116–17, 118, 118–19, 120, 122, 124, 127–8, 162, 164–5, 165, 180
    dry-stone 21, 22, 24, 25, 26–7
    paths 26–7, 35, 36–7, 38, 38–9
    paving 32–3, 36, 40, 41, 46, 49, 60–1, 64, 70, 72–3, 90, 90–1, 92, 93, 124, 124–7, 127, 170, 175
    sculptures 35, 36–7, 43–4, 45, 72, 74–5
Surrealism 16, 22, 23, 159
swimming pools 12, 154, 154–5, 172–5

T
Takano, Fumiaki 60–5
"Takapuna, Garden at" at 102–5
"Theatre of Light" 94–7
"Theatre of the Trees" 107, 120–3
Tijou, Jean 72
tiles 62, 110, 124, 125, 127, 128–9, 144–5, 150, 172, 172–3
Tinguely, Jean 45, 86, 88
Toll, Julie 180–3
"Touched by Wind" 81, 98–101
"Touchy-Feely Garden, The" 46–9
Trianon, le Grand see Versailles
Tschumi, Bernard 10, 16
Tunnard, Christopher 15
Turf Parterre 142
Turner, Richard 9
Turturiello, Pompeo 35, 36–7

V
van der Rohe, Mies 109
van Sweden, James 165
Versailles 8, 13, 15, 143
Villa Aldobrandini, Frascati 13

Villa Belvedere, Rome 108
Villa Cicogna Mozzoni, Bisuchio 108
Villa d'Este, Tivoli 82, 84–5
Villa Medici, Fiesole 120
Villa Orsini, Bomarzo 22
Villa Quaracchi, Florence 120–2
Villaroya and Theisen 34–35
Vivant, Pierre 22
Vitruvius 120
Voegele, Harald 35, 36–7
"Voyage of Vitality" 4, 5, 157, 162–5

W
Watanabe, Makato Sei 81, 98–101
water 15, 22, 24–7, 28–30, 31, 36, 46–8, 57, 70, 83, 84–5, 86–9, 90, 92, 94, 94–6, 98–100, 116–18, 118–19, 124–7, 127, 128, 128–9, 134, 162–5, 166–7, 168–9, 170–1, 180–3, 186
    see also fountains
Wirtz, Jacques 176
wood 14–15, 24, 26–7, 42, 44, 45, 94, 96, 134, 144–6, 146–7, 148, 148–9, 176, 176–7, 178, 182–3
Woodhams, Stephen 112–15

Y, Z
Young, John 56–7, 59
Zen gardens 50–1, 52, 53, 86–9, 100

PHOTOGRAPHIC ACKNOWLEDGMENTS

The publisher would like to thank the following for their kind permission to reproduce the photographs in this book.

Front Cover: Paul Cooper/Marianne Majerus; Back Cover: Helen Fickling/The Interior Archive; Back inside flap: Paul Cooper endpapers: Stephen Jerrom, Glass Garden Inc., www.glassgardendesign.com/Nicola Browne; 1: Chaumont-sur-Loire, Conservatoire/Deidi von Schaewen; 2: Robin Winogrond; 5: Designer: Bonita Bulaitis/Christopher-Poole Associates; 7: Nigel Francis/Robert Harding Picture Library; 8: AKG London; 9: Garden Matters; 10: Elvaston Castle Country Park and Estate Museum, Derbyshire; 11: Nigel Francis/Robert Harding Picture Library; 12 Designer: Thomas Church/Garden Matters; 13 right: Advertising Archives; 13 left: Advertising Archives; 14 above: The Works of Naum Gabo, Nina Williams/Christie's Images, Ltd; 14 below: Neil Beer/Corbis; 15: Designer: Roberto Burle Marx/Noel Kingsbury; 16: Hugh Rooney/Eye Ubiquitous/Corbis; 17: Office of Dan Kiley, Vermont/Photo: Aaron Kiley; 19: Designer: Christopher Bradley-Hole/Marianne Majerus; 20: Copyright Succession Marcel Duchamp/ADAGP, Paris and DACS, London 2000; 21 above: Deidi von Schaewen; 21 below: Photograph by Jean-Marc Pharisien, Andy Goldsworthy from his book *Stone* (Viking/Abrams, 1994); 22: Ruggero Vanni/Corbis; 23: Designer: Ivan Hicks/Andrew Lawson; 25: Designer: Christopher Bradley-Hole/Marianne Majerus; 26 above: Designer: Christopher Bradley-Hole/Andrea Jones/Garden Exposures Photo Library; 26 below: Designer: Christopher Bradley-Hole/Marianne Majerus; 27: Designer: Christopher Bradley-Hole/Courtesy of *The Daily Telegraph*; 28: David Stevens; 29: David Stevens; 30: David Stevens; 31: David Stevens; 32 left: Architect: Georg Hermann, Munich/Mariposa; 32–33: Mariposa/Roland Halbe/Artur; 34: Mariposa/Roland Halbe/Artur; 35: Mariposa/Roland Halbe/Artur; 36 left: Mariposa/Roland Halbe/Artur; 36–37: Mariposa/Roland Halbe/Artur; 38–39: T Delaney Inc.; 40–41: T Delaney Inc.; 42–43: Designer: Speckhardt/Andrea Jones/Garden Exposures Photo Library; 44 right: Designer: Speckhardt/Andrew Lawson; 44 left: Designer: Speckhardt/Andrea Jones/Garden Exposures Photo Library; 45: Designer: Speckhardt/Andrew Jones; 46–47: Designer: Emily Ault/Magali Delporte; 48–49: Designer: Emily Ault/Magali Delporte; 50–51: Martha Schwartz Inc./Photo: Alan Ward; 52–53: Martha Schwartz Inc./Photo: Alan Ward; 55: Dean Cardasis & Associates, Amherst, MA; 56: Designer: Shiro Kuramata/Vitra Ltd; 57: David Stevens; 58: Designer: Dan Pearson/Peter Baistow; 59: Architect: John Young/Richard Bryant/Arcaid; 60–61: Takano Landscape Planning/Andrea Jones/Garden Exposures Photo Library; 62–63: Takano Landscape Planning/Andrea Jones/Garden Exposures Photo Library; 64–65: Takano Landscape Planning/Andrea Jones/Garden Exposures Photo Library; 66–67: Schaudt Architekten/Reiner Blunck; 68–69: Schaudt Architekten/Reiner Blunck; 70–71: Designer Michael Balston/Andrea Jones/Garden Exposures Photo Library; 71 above: Courtesy of Michael Balston; 72: Designer Michael Balston/Clive Nichols; 73: Designer Michael Balston/Steven Wooster; 74–75: Designer Michael Balston/Clive Nichols; 76–77: Dean Cardasis & Associates, Amherst, MA; 78–79: Dean Cardasis & Associates, Amherst, MA; 81: Makato Sei Watanabe, Japan; 82: Mike Newton/Robert Harding Picture Library; 83 left: Advertising Archives; 83 right: Octopus Publishing Group; 84: ADAGP, Paris and DACS, London 2000/Philip James Corwin/Corbis; 85: Martha Schwartz Inc./Nicola Browne; 86: Chaumont-sur-Loire, Conservatoire; 87: Helen Fickling/The Interior Archive; 88–89: Helen Fickling/The Interior Archive; 94–95: Highwater Jones Ltd, Isle of Wight; 96–97: Highwater Jones Ltd, Isle of Wight; 98–99: Makato Sei Watanabe, Japan; 100–101: Makato Sei Watanabe, Japan; 102–103: Ted Smyth/Steven Wooster; 104–105: Ted Smyth/Steven Wooster; 107: Antoine Predock Architect/Timothy Hursley; 108: David Markson/Octopus Publishing Group; 109: Billie Love Historical Collection; 110; above: Architect: Steven Ehrlich/Photo: Sonia Fonseca; 110 below: Designer: Dan Pearson/Nicola Browne; 111: Architect: Enrique Browne & Borja Huidobro/Photo: Guy Wenborne; 113: Designer: Stephen Woodhams/Geoff Howard; 114: Courtesy of Stephen Woodhams; 115: Designer: Stephen Woodhams/Geoff Howard; 116–117: Antoine Predock Architect/Timothy Hursley; 118–119: Antoine Predock Architect/Timothy Hursley; 120–121: Antoine Predock Architect/Timothy Hursley; 122: Courtesy of Antoine Predock Architect; 123: Antoine Predock Architect/Timothy Hursley; 124–125: Designer: Rod Barnett/Steven Wooster; 126: Designer: Rod Barnett/Steven Wooster 128–129: Designer: Rod Barnett/Steven Wooster; 130: Courtesy of Batter Kay Associates; 131: Architect: Batter Kay Associates/Jeremy Samuelson; 132: Architect: Batter Kay Associates/Jeremy Samuelson; 134–135: Niall McLaughlin Architects/Nicholas Kane/Arcaid; 136–137: Niall McLaughlin Architects/Nicholas Kane/Arcaid; 136 below: Courtesy of Niall McLaughlin Architects; 139: Martha Schwartz Inc.; 140 above: Octopus Publishing Group; 140–142: Peter Kukorelli; 142: Chaumont-sur-Loire, Conservatoire/Deidi von Schaewen; 143: Mara Adamitz Scrupe/Photo Daniel J Holm; 144: Chaumont-sur-Loire, Conservatoire; 145: Chaumont-sur-Loire, Conservatoire/Harpur Garden Library; 146: Chaumont-sur-Loire, Conservatoire; 147: Chaumont-sur-Loire, Conservatoire/Photo: Christophe Fillioux; 149: Designer: Bonita Bulaitis/John Glover/Garden Picture Library; 150–151: Designer: Bonita Bulaitis/Jill Billington; 152: Martha Schwartz Inc.; 153: Martha Schwartz Inc./Michael Blier; 154: Martha Schwartz Inc./Michael Blier; 155: Martha Schwartz Inc.; 157: Designer: Bonita Bulaitis/Christopher-Poole Associates; 158: Designer: Paul Cooper/Christopher-Poole Associates; 159: Colourscape/Martin Beddall/Rex Features; 160: Designer: Martha Schwartz Inc./Nicola Browne; 161: Christo and Jeanne-Claude/W Volz/Bilderberg/Network; 162–163: Designer: Bonita Bulaitis/Christopher-Poole Associates; 164: Designer: Bonita Bulaitis/Christopher-Poole Associates; 166–167: Stephen Jerrom, Glass Garden Inc., www.glassgardendesign.com /Nicola Browne; 168 above: Stephen Jerrom, Glass Garden Inc., www.glassgardendesign.com; 168 below: Designer: Stephen Jerrom, Glass Garden Inc., www.glassgardendesign.com/Nicola Browne; 170–171: Designer: Stephen Jerrom, Glass Garden Inc., www.glassgardendesign.com /Nicola Browne; 172–173: Designer: Mia Lehrer/Steven A Gunther Photography; 174–175: Designer: Mia Lehrer/Steven A Gunther Photography; 177: Chaumont-sur-Loire, Conservatoire; 178–179: Chaumont-sur-Loire, Conservatoire; 181: Designers: Julie Toll, Nordstrom, Oskarsson/Clive Nichols 182–183: Designers: Julie Toll, Nordstrom, Oskarsson/Clive Nichols; 184: Designer: Paul Cooper/Marianne Majerus; 185: Courtesy of Paul Cooper; 186–187: Designer: Paul Cooper/Marianne Majerus; 188–189: Designer: Paul Cooper/Marianne Majerus.